THE BEAT FLEET

THE BEAT FLEET

THE STORY BEHIND THE 60's 'PIRATE' RADIO STATIONS

Mike Leonard

FOREST PRESS (HESWALL)

ISBN 0 9527684 1 0

© Mike Leonard 2004

First published 2004

Printed in Great Britain by
RCS plc, Randall Park Way, Retford DN22 7WF

Published by
Forest Press (Heswall), P O Box 1, Heswall, Wirral, CH60 3TH, England

British Library Cataloguing-in-Publication Data
A catalogue record for this book is available from the British Library

By the same author
From International Waters - 60 Years of Offshore Broadcasting
(ISBN 0 9527684 0 2) 1996, Reprinted 1997

Acknowledgements

Many people and organisations have provided assistance in collating information for this book, which also draws on earlier research undertaken for the author's other publication on offshore radio – *From International Waters – 60 Years of Offshore Broadcasting.*

Thousands of source documents were studied during the course of this research and my thanks go to those un-named people who produced contemporary publications and records chronicling the life and events surrounding the offshore radio stations.

Pictures used in this book are from the author's personal archive, including the series published in the 1960s by the former Free Radio Association, but because that organisation disappeared many years ago it has not been possible, unfortunately, to establish who took the actual pictures. Nevertheless I record my thanks to them.

Former listeners were good enough to supply their personal reminiscences of different aspects of the offshore stations and many of these contributions appear in the following pages under the generic title 'Vox Pop'. Thank you to everyone who took the time and trouble to put their memories down on paper. They provide a unique insight into the everyday impact of the offshore stations on those who listened to them.

Finally, but most importantly, I would like to thank all those who owned or worked on the offshore radio stations, providing entertainment pleasure for millions of people. This book is a tribute to their work.

Introduction

They were called pirates, but they weren't even illegal, just operating from bases outside British territorial waters – offshore. Even after legislation was introduced the stations themselves were not illegal, it was the (British) people who aided or worked for them who broke the law.

Whatever terminology you want to use – pirate or offshore - the stations based on ships and derelict forts off the coast, and those who broadcast from them, brought pleasure to millions of people. They operated for four years in the mid 60's at a time when huge social and economic changes were taking place in Britain. As well as being an outlet for the wealth of new music talent which was emerging so rapidly during those years the offshore stations also provided the musical background for everything else that was happening in the country.

People enjoyed their informality and spontaneity as well as their whole new approach to radio entertainment, not just providing music all day, but jingles, commercials, regular short news bulletins, competitions and the general camaraderie generated by a group of people living and working together, in a restricted space, for weeks at a time.

For the first time in British radio history DJs spoke to their audience, not at them. Listeners in return felt an empathy for the stations, sharing in the ups and downs of everyday life on board the ships or forts.

But behind the public image offshore radio was a competitive business, with profits to be made and market shares to capture. Many offshore stations didn't achieve either, but others did – and very successfully. The behind-the-scenes story of rivalry and competition, with its real life struggles, dramas and even tragedies is as fascinating as the sound of the stations themselves.

Mike Leonard

March 2004

Contents

Chapter 1   What State radio did for us..............1

Chapter 2   Your all day music station...............9

Chapter 3   Rivals, Friends and Forts..............17

Chapter 4   Competition and Goodguys............27

Chapter 5   The flotilla sails in........................33

Chapter 6   Expansion and Tragedy................45

Chapter 7   Outlawed...................................57

Chapter 8   The fight for Free Radio................63

Chapter 9   Scuppered!................................77

Chapter 10   ...and the beat goes on.................89

Appendix 1   The ships................................97

Appendix 2   The Sea Forts...........................98

Bibliography..100

Some Useful Addresses...............................101

Index...102

"This is Radio Caroline on 199, your all day music station".

With these words, first broadcast on 28th March 1964 the arrival of music radio, available on demand, all day, every day became a reality and the BBC's monopoly on sound broadcasting to Britain was broken. Now listeners had a choice, limited by today's standards, but nevertheless a major stride forward 40 years ago.

Today, musical entertainment is available everywhere you go – supermarkets, hotels, shopping malls, personal stereos, the internet, TV music channels and, of course, a plethora of local, regional and national radio stations.

But it wasn't always like that. 40 years ago if you wanted to listen to your favourite music you bought (vinyl) records and played them on a gramophone or a state-of-the-art hi-fi unit – essentially 'pieces of furniture' located permanently in one room of your home. There were a few, very few, half hour television music programmes such as "6-5 Special", "Thank Your Lucky Stars" and "Juke Box Jury"; there was some limited music available on the radio from three national BBC stations; and during the evening the ever-fading signal of Radio Luxembourg. That was it.

Place this in the context of the early 60's growth in music and youth culture, the emergence of Merseybeat and 'Swinging London' and you can begin to imagine

(remember?) how frustrating it was to have to wait until a specific day and time to listen to your favourite music – unless of course you could afford to assemble a large record collection of your own and have unlimited access to that 'piece of furniture' – no personal stereos or mini systems in your bedroom, remember!

It is not that people didn't want to listen to music at any time of the day that suited them (although some did resent the intrusion of 'pop' music into their everyday life), the opportunity was simply not there. With such a latent demand for music to be available 'on tap' all day it was inevitable that, sooner or later, someone would come along and fill that gap, but it wasn't going to be either of the existing radio broadcasters.

The BBC, who held a monopoly on radio broadcasting in Britain, didn't fully understand or appreciate the gap in the market left by their existing services. There was a culture in the organisation that thought continuous pop music programmes would be irrelevant, vulgar and at odds with the Corporation's public service role to 'educate and inform'.

As well as fulfilling this public service role imposed by its charter the BBC was restricted in other ways from expanding its broadcast output. All programmes had to be financed from revenue generated through the Licence Fee system and commercial advertising was

Vox Pop

I first heard Radio Caroline as the ship sailed towards the Isle of Man. Some people at school had heard it already and I went home to try and tune in my Dad's radio before he came home from work. Radio Caroline was hardly ever off after that.

Peter (Blackpool, Lancashire)

Radio London was like nothing else we had ever heard. I had listened to Radio Caroline almost from the beginning, but when Radio London came on - WOW - it was so different, so professional, so lively. I retuned to 266 and never heard Caroline again - until Big L had closed!

Maureen (Hornchurch, Essex)

absolutely not allowed to be broadcast on the Corporation's television and radio services. Additionally, trade restrictions imposed by the music and record industry limited the number of records which could be played by the BBC during their programmes. To a certain extent the BBC did try to get around the music industry's 'needle time' restrictions by employing musicians and artists to perform live cover versions of current hits as well as standard classics from the dance band era, but for the majority of listeners these were poor substitutes for the real artists.

For example, the BBC Light Programme, provided listeners with a total of less than four hours a week of pop music with "Saturday Club" and the Sunday afternoon chart programme "Pick of the Pops". There were a number of other music-based programmes on the BBC at the time -"The Jack Jackson Show", "Housewive's Choice", "Two Way Family Favourites", "Midday Spin" and of course "Uncle Mac's Children's Favourites". Much of the output in these programmes contained either live cover versions by session musicians or many 'hardy annual' records which cropped up again and again in listener's requests. Who can forget "The Runaway Train", "The Laughing Policeman", "Nellie the Elephant", "Woody Woodpecker" and other regular 'favourites'?

The other broadcaster whose programmes drew a significant British audience was the commercially funded Radio Luxembourg – 'The Station of the Stars'. Their English Service programmes were beamed from a transmitter located in the central European principality – the only legal way they could operate without infringing the BBC's monopoly position in Britain.

English Service transmissions from Luxembourg took place only during the evening, when the other language services had finished. They started around 7.00 pm and ended at 1.00 or 2.00 am, but the under-powered medium wave (AM) signal on 208m was prone to frequent and regular fading, often lasting for two or three minutes at a time, dependant on atmospheric and weather conditions prevalent at the time of year.

Despite these technical problems the English Service of Radio Luxembourg had been popular with British listeners since it had returned to the air after the Second World War. It supplied general entertainment programmes as well as music, with a more relaxed style of presentation than the BBC.

During the 1950's Radio Luxembourg's output was based on sponsored shows, with programme content being dictated by the sponsor. For example a typical evening schedule would contain a number of 15 or 30 minute programmes such as "The Cliff Richard Show" (music), "The Sporting Challenge" (in which listener's questions about sporting achievements and records were put to Memory Man, Leslie Welch), "Italy Sings" (Italian music), "Record Crop" (music), "Bringing Christ to the Nations" (religious broadcast) and "Spin With the Stars" (music).

After the arrival of commercial television in Britain in 1955 many of Luxembourg's entertainment programmes such as "Take Your Pick", "Double Your Money" and "Opportunity Knocks" - and much of the consumer advertising that went with them - were diverted to the new ITV stations. By 1959 the station had changed its output to target the newly identified 'teenage market' and dispensed with all the light entertainment programmes, replacing them with pop music shows.

One serious side effect of this change in policy was that sponsors became more difficult to find so Radio Luxembourg filled this void by negotiating package deals with various record companies to buy large amounts of airtime on the station. Gradually the major record companies, Decca, Pye, EMI and Phillips took over the station and its programming, effectively block-booking airtime to promote their records, which were rarely played in full - to squeeze as many as possible into a 15 or 30 minute sponsored programme.

By the early 1960s, with such a stranglehold on its airtime, the English Service of Radio Luxembourg, although it claimed to be a leader of the musical revolution, had effectively become just a marketing tool of the major record labels.

While British audiences had to content themselves with what was on offer from the BBC and Radio Luxembourg, in Europe during the late 1950's and early 1960s, challengers to the public service broadcasting monopolies began to appear. These were commercially funded stations based on board ships anchored in international waters outside territorial boundaries, providing entertainment and alternative programming not generally available on the state run networks. The programmes were not always just continuous music, some of the early offshore stations also attempted to provide a range of talk and entertainment programmes in addition to popular music.

The reason why these new stations operated from offshore bases was to circumvent restrictions placed on all established broadcasters – frequencies were allocated by international treaty and individual national governments determined who was to be allowed to use those frequencies. Any potential challengers to the 'authorised' broadcasters would not be granted licences to establish stations, and anyway in many countries, commercially funded radio and television was considered to be politically and socially unacceptable and often perceived as being responsible for lowering broadcasting standards.

The Scandinavian countries were the first to experience this new phenomenon. Radio Mercur was established off the Danish coast in July 1958, followed in March 1961 by Radio Nord off the Swedish coast. Both of these stations provided popular music programmes, challenging their respective state broadcasters' mundane output. Radio Nord in particular introduced to Europe the American Top 40 music and news style of programming, based on the success of station KLIF in Dallas, whose pioneering owner, Gordon McLendon, was employed to advise the Swedish station on programme format.

An attempt was made by another offshore station, in September 1961, to provide more varied programmes for its audience as an alternative to continuous pop music. DCR (Danmarks Commercialle Radio) was established by a breakaway group from Radio Mercur and their station produced programmes of classical music, operas, plays and discussions in addition to 'light' music. However DCR was not a commercial success and it merged with Radio Mercur in January 1962, providing that station with a second ship to increase its coverage of Denmark's radio audience.

Another offshoot of Radio Mercur came on the air in April 1962 – Radio Syd, broadcasting to southern Sweden. This station had started by buying airtime on Radio Mercur, but eventually acquired its own ship and became a full time Swedish language station, under the ownership of Britt Wadner, formerly head of sales at Radio Mercur.

However, by July 1962 the Scandinavian governments had all introduced legislation to ban offshore broadcasting and prevent their nationals taking part in, or advertising on, such stations. Radio Mercur and Radio Nord both closed before the legislation came into effect, but Britt Wadner decided to defy the new law and Radio Syd continued to broadcast for another three and a half years, despite her being prosecuted and imprisoned and advertisers being fined for buying airtime on the station.

Holland and Belgium too saw challenges to their established broadcasting systems from offshore-based stations. Radio Veronica began broadcasting to Holland in April 1960 and quickly established itself as a popular alternative to the Dutch national radio system. In neighbouring Belgium, Radio Antwerpen came on the air in October 1962 and similarly provided a popular alternative to the state broadcaster. Unfortunately this station was only a short-lived success as its ship ran aground in December 1962 after breaking its anchor chain and drifting during a storm.

With the experience of these successful challenges in Europe an attempt was made in the early 1960s to broadcast alternative radio services to Britain from an offshore base. Radio Veronica experimented with an English language service – CNBC (Commercial Neutral Broadcasting Company) - in 1962, but this was discontinued after a few weeks of test broadcasts because of poor reception and greater demand from advertisers in Holland for airtime on the Dutch language station.

The emergence of a strong British music industry in the early 1960's forced the pace for the more widespread provision of pop music programmes on radio. The BBC did very little, if anything, to respond to this growth, relying on its outdated agreement with the Musicians Union which restricted the amount of 'needle time' (time allocated to playing records during broadcasts) to 24 hours a week, spread over its three national networks. Radio Luxembourg tried to respond, but had its own problems - its agreements with record companies effectively tied up most of its airtime, it was geographically isolated from the source of the new music revolution, still having no direct landline facilities between its London studios and the transmitters in Europe, and it only broadcast during the evenings.

Into this scenario came a number of businessmen who saw a potential market for an all day pop music station and who had witnessed the success of similar projects in Scandinavia and Holland. The time seemed ripe to launch an offshore radio station to serve Britain.

The first public announcement of such a project appeared in October 1961 after John Thompson, a journalist from Slough, and Robert Collier, a wholesale newsagent, formed a radio broadcasting company - The Voice of Slough Ltd. Technical adviser to the project was Arnold Swanson, a Canadian millionaire who had made his fortune from the invention and manufacture of car safety belts.

A 70 ton fishing vessel, *Ellen,* was said to have been purchased and fitted out in Scotland with an on-air date for the station planned for 1st December 1961. Although registered as the Voice of Slough the station had a number of proposed call-signs including Radio LN (Ellen), Radio ELB and GBLN (Great Britain, Ellen or Great Britain, London).

The project's radio ship was to be anchored not far from the Nore lightship off the Essex coast near Southend and programmes were to be pre-recorded either in 'studios' located in two wooden huts at the rear of a cottage in Aylesbury or in a 30' caravan which had been equipped as a mobile studio facility.

The 24 hour format was, according to the station's publicity material, to be "musical and directed mainly at the young, with regular news commentaries and current affairs programmes throughout the day." John Thompson also hinted that broadcasting facilities could be used to provide a local community station directed at Southend and claimed to have support from the Mayor of the town for such a venture.

voice of slough ltd.
35 BEECHWOOD GDNS.
SLOUGH

Keith Martin, an announcer who had worked with Paul Hollingdale and Doug Stanley at the short-lived Radio Veronica English service, CNBC and who later went on to become involved with Radio Atlanta and Radio Caroline, recorded some programmes for the proposed station in the Aylesbury cottage studios. But despite initial publicity the proposed starting date for the station came and went with nothing being heard on the airwaves.

The project reportedly floundered when record companies refused to allow the station to infringe copyright restrictions by tape recording discs for later broadcast. However, correspondence from John Thompson exists which indicates that as late as September 1962 he was still pursuing plans to launch his offshore station, under the call-sign GBLN. In that correspondence he claimed the ship was being held up by British Customs authorities on a technicality, but that he was trying to free her from "red tape" and put the station on air by mid-October 1962.

At about the same time that the Voice of Slough (or GBLN) was due to come on air in December 1961, the project had lost its technical adviser, Arnold Swanson. He had decided instead to launch his own offshore station - GBOK (Great Britain OK) - from an 84 year old former lightship, the *Lady*

Dixon, which he claimed to have purchased. This wooden vessel, which was re-registered in Liberia, had been built in 1878 to serve as a lightship off the north west coast of Ireland.

The Amalgamated Broadcasting Company was formed to front the project with registered offices and studios at Swanson's home, Notley Abbey, Thame, Buckinghamshire. Swanson converted the stables of this large house into recording studios and established a London office to sell commercial airtime through another company, Adanac Broadcasting Agency.

Announcer Ed Moreno (who was later to work for several offshore radio stations) spent four days a week for several months recording GBOK programmes at the Notley Abbey studios. American Evangelist Ted Armstrong (whose programmes were also heard on many later British offshore stations) bought airtime on GBOK and even announced the station's forthcoming launch in some of his publicity literature.

The first press reports about GBOK appeared in February 1962, indicating that at the end of the month the station would start broadcasting music, features and advertising 24 hours a day from a vessel anchored near The Nore lightship, the same location as had been planned for the Voice of Slough's broadcasting ship.

The station planned to reach a potential audience of 11 million listeners within a 150 mile radius covering the south east and Midlands. Places as far away as Nottingham, Leicester, Coventry, Birmingham and Bristol

were estimated to be within the station's primary coverage area and a "bonus French audience" across the English Channel was also offered for the benefit of advertisers.

GBOK was promoted in a glossy 12 page brochure which attempted to explain in some detail to listeners and potential advertisers (who were accustomed only to the BBC's style of programming) just what a 24 hour American format music station would sound like.

Programmes were to be of popular music with five minute news broadcasts on the hour every hour - a completely new experience for British listeners who were used to the BBC's diet of early morning, lunchtime and evening 'set piece' news bulletins. GBOK planned to make the claim "First with the Important News" for this service.

After the early morning "Wake-up Show" ended at 9.00am another new programming concept was proposed. Known as "Bandwheel", this show (an internationally copyrighted programme to which GBOK had exclusive British rights) was scheduled to run for 10 hours each day. It would be interrupted only by news on the hour and a two hour "Motorway Special" between 4.00pm and 6.00pm each evening, recognising the then new and growing market for drive-time listeners - commuters with radios in their cars.

Between the hours of 10.00pm and 6.30am GBOK planned the "All Night Dance Party", with sponsors being sought for each hourly segment or even the complete night's programme. Newscasts could also be sponsored at the station's basic 5 minute rate plus a 33% premium and by March 1962 Arnold Swanson was claiming to have already sold enough airtime to finance a complete year's programming on GBOK.

However, the station's planned on air date had to be postponed when, at the end of February 1962 an unexpected problem was encountered. The *Lady Dixon* (which some press reports suggested had been renamed *The Bucaneer*) was moored at a wharf in a muddy creek at Pitsea in the Thames Estuary. Sailing the vessel from this mooring depended on high spring tides reaching Pitsea and flooding the creek. Unfortunately for GBOK the first spring tide did not prove to be high enough to float the *Lady Dixon*, which became stuck on a mudbank. Attempts by two tugs to release the ship failed because only one end could be raised from what was fast becoming a mud cradle around the ex-lightship's wooden hull, so it was decided to wait for the next high tide at the beginning of March.

It was not until 9th March that the *Lady Dixon* was successfully refloated and towed to Sheerness for final fitting out. National publicity for GBOK appeared in *The Times* the following day reporting that once machinery and transmitting equipment had been installed the vessel would be towed to her position in

international waters and broadcasting would commence "within two weeks". The vessel arrived at Sheerness on 12th March for fitting out, however, it is unclear whether this was ever completed, although there are reports of an unofficial test transmission having been made from the *Lady Dixon* whilst in port, resulting in a raid by Post Office officials.

By July 1962 Arnold Swanson announced that work on the *Lady Dixon* was to be abandoned as she was no longer considered sufficiently seaworthy for her role as a radio ship. Altogether over £15,000 had been lost on work associated with converting the ageing vessel, but undaunted by this setback Swanson said that he had now acquired an ex-Tank Landing Craft which would be turned into a radio ship. The new craft was to have a stronger transmitter, giving a projected coverage area as far north as Manchester, and

although Swanson claimed that GBOK would start broadcasting from its new vessel by September 1962, the station never appeared on the air.

Despite the non-appearance of either GBLN or GBOK the idea of operating an English language offshore radio station had not been lost completely.

Australian music publisher, Allan Crawford, had established Merit Music Publishing in London in 1960, managing minor artists and producing cover versions of hit songs on his own record labels - Rocket, Sabre and Carnival. His philosophy was simple - he thought that increased record sales - and consequently Top 20 chart listings - could best be achieved by repeatedly promoting artists and record labels to the largest possible audience

In 1962 Allan Crawford rented some new office accommodation, which by coincidence was in the building vacated by the recently defunct CNBC project. Reputedly it was whilst clearing out papers and promotional material left by the previous occupants that Crawford realised the potential for starting an offshore radio station broadcasting to an English speaking audience. In keeping with his business philosophy, he knew that if he started a radio station of his own he would have the means to endlessly promote his company's record labels and artists to a large audience.

He set about convincing a number of wealthy and influential backers of the commercial potential for launching an offshore radio station to challenge the BBC's monopoly. The result was the formation of Project Atlanta Ltd., which initially had 38 separate investors each holding anything between just 50 and 10,000 of the company's 150,000 shares.

Allan Crawford had closely followed the fortunes of the Scandinavian offshore stations and was aware that nearly all were about to close because of new legislation to outlaw them during the summer of 1962. He negotiated a deal with the American backers of Radio Nord to purchase that station's vessel, *Magda Maria*, complete and ready to broadcast, together with the entire contents of the fully equipped land-based studios in

Stockholm. In addition Crawford was interested in taking on some of the Radio Nord technical staff and marine crew to continue operating the *Magda Maria* and all its equipment.

After Radio Nord had closed the *Magda Maria* docked at El Ferrol in northern Spain at the beginning of August 1962 where a complete overhaul of the vessel took place and the renovated ship left port in mid September, giving her destination as Dover, England. A few days later she dropped anchor in the Thames Estuary, but unfortunately during the time that the *Magda Maria* had been in dock the Danish authorities had boarded and seized another Scandinavian offshore radio ship, the former Radio Mercur vessel *Lucky Star*.

Following the closure of Radio Mercur on 31st July 1962 one of its ships, *Lucky Star*, remained at sea and on 13th August transmissions were once again started using some old programme tapes. The original Radio Mercur owners denied responsibility for these transmissions and stated that during the life of the station they had only ever hired the ship from the vessel's owner in Guatemala through an associate company.

Two days later armed Danish police boarded the *Lucky Star*, amidst reports that there had been a murder on board. As the ship apparently had no official registration (the Lebanese flag flying from her stern was a fake) a customs vessel escorted her into port and she was impounded until her owners appeared and the registration irregularities had been cleared up.

Although a court subsequently ruled that the boarding and seizure of the *Lucky Star* in international waters was legal because she was stateless the apparent deliberate flouting of international maritime law by the Danish authorities in forcibly boarding what, at the time, appeared to be a foreign-registered ship anchored outside their territorial limits had the effect of frightening off some of Allan Crawford's financial backers. They feared that the British authorities may well do the same to the *Magda Maria* now lying at anchor in the Thames Estuary and withdrew their funding from Project Atlanta.

With the *Magda Maria* off the British coast, fully equipped and ready to start broadcasting,

Crawford tried to renegotiate the deal with the vessel's owners, Radio Nord, in an effort to keep Project Atlanta alive. He suggested that they should give him what amounted to a credit arrangement so that Project Atlanta would lease the *Magda Maria* until the station had been broadcasting for some time and the attitude of the British authorities had become clearer. This way, if the ship was seized and confiscated, Project Atlanta would only incur minimal financial losses.

The owners, on the other hand, wanted the refurbished ship paid for in full before broadcasting began so that if the vessel were seized by the British authorities they would not lose financially or be responsible in any way for the detained vessel. Unable to agree a compromise both parties stood their ground and finally the deal between Radio Nord and Project Atlanta was called off.

In early October 1962 the *Magda Maria*, sailed from the Thames Estuary and dropped anchor off the coast of Holland, near the Radio Veronica ship *Borkum Riff.* Although the deal with Project Atlanta had fallen through the ship's owners were willing to wait a short while longer for Allan Crawford to try and secure alternative sources of funding. However, at the same time other possible purchasers were also being sought.

The Dutch and Belgian press at the time speculated about various plans for the ship, including a claim by a Dutch businessman that he would purchase her either to launch a second Dutch offshore station (to compete with Radio Veronica) or to establish a station off the British coast. There were also suggestions that the vessel would be used to house a television station beaming programmes to Belgium.

Another rumour circulating was that the ship had been sold to the Cuban Government for use as a propaganda station anchored off the United States coast. This particular story had some credibility because it circulated at the time of the Cuban Missile Crisis, which posed the first real threat to world peace since the end of the Second World War. US President John F Kennedy was involved in a standoff with Premier Kruschev of the USSR over the build-up of Soviet missiles on the island of Cuba, all provocatively directed towards

America. It is quite conceivable that, at that time, the Communist Government of Cuba, backed by the USSR, would have wished to use an offshore radio station as a base from which to pump propaganda into America.

After about three weeks lying at anchor the *Magda Maria* entered Ostend Harbour in late October 1962 where she remained while rumours continued to be published in the European press about her future. However, they all came to nothing and speculation about the future of the vessel died down.

Throughout this period the *Magda Maria* was still in the ownership of the Radio Nord organisation and the sale of the vessel was being handled through a series of agents and companies based in various central European countries. By 11th January 1963 the vessel, which had now been renamed *Mi Amigo*, was recorded as entering Flushing Harbour and details supplied to the authorities show that she was then owned by a company called Amatara, with an address in Liechtenstein.

Having been unable to sell the vessel as a fully equipped radio station, the ship's owners decided to sail the *Mi Amigo* across the Atlantic to Texas where it was planned to remove all the radio equipment and convert her into a luxury cruiser for recreational use by members of the former Radio Nord consortium.

Accordingly the *Mi Amigo* set sail from Brest on 26th January, calling at Las Palmas en route before arriving in Galveston, Texas on 9th March. There are some unsubstantiated reports that the ship was used briefly at this time to broadcast programmes from the Gulf of Mexico before finally having her transmitting mast removed.

Meanwhile, Allan Crawford had not given up his plan to launch a British offshore radio station and throughout 1963 he sought to obtain new sources of funding for Project Atlanta. By December he had succeeded and the *Mi Amigo* was finally purchased by Project Atlanta from the former Radio Nord consortium. Luckily that consortium's plans to strip all radio equipment from the vessel and fit her out as a luxury cruiser had not been fully implemented, (only the transmitting mast and rigging had been removed) so with the transfer of ownership finalised, the *Mi Amigo*

set sail from Galveston on 28th December, heading once again towards the British coast.

The *Mi Amigo* arrived in Las Palmas at the end of January 1964, after encountering heavy Atlantic storms, during which she nearly sank, and on 5th February she entered El Ferrol once again for repairs, ballasting and strengthening of her hull. These works were completed within 10 days and the ship sailed, docking at Corunna until 3rd March, while Allan Crawford desperately made arrangements to try and find a quiet port in which the *Mi Amigo* could be fitted with a new transmitter mast to continue her role as a floating radio station.

Chapter 2   Your all day music station

Allan Crawford was not the only person proposing to launch a British offshore radio station in 1963. Another plan was being hatched by Ronan O'Rahilly the son of a wealthy Irish businessman who had operated the Preston-Greenore ferry service on behalf of British Railways and purchased the port of Greenore when that service was discontinued.

Then 23 years old, Ronan O'Rahilly had come to London in the late 1950s and joined Studio 57, a 'method acting' school. In the early 1960s he had also become involved in running the Scene Club in Great Windmill Street and managing groups such as Blues Incorporated, whose members included Mick Jagger and Charlie Watts, later of the Rolling Stones.

It was in this role of manager/record promoter that, in 1962 Ronan O'Rahilly met with senior executives of Radio Luxembourg in London to ask if they would give air-play to one of his artists, Georgie Fame. He was told that Radio Luxembourg could not do this because the major record companies bought virtually all the station's airtime and they decided what was played during each programme. Faced with this situation Ronan O'Rahilly concluded that the only way to secure airtime for artists who were not signed by the major record companies, would be to start a radio station himself.

At first he explored the possibility of hiring the transmitters of a foreign based broadcaster, but after becoming aware of the success of offshore radio in Scandinavia and Holland, rejected this option in favour of using a ship anchored outside British territorial limits to launch his own station.

Ronan O'Rahilly met Allan Crawford of Project Atlanta through a group of mutual acquaintances and the offshore radio station idea was discussed by the two men. Crawford was already well advanced with his plans, but he had suffered a setback with the loss of financial backing for Project Atlanta and consequently the purchase of the radio ship, *Mi Amigo*. It was suggested that they could co-operate and launch two offshore radio stations - one to serve the south east of England (to be operated by Crawford) and the

other to serve northern England and Ireland (operated by O'Rahilly).

As part of his planning for Project Atlanta Allan Crawford had commissioned technical and market research which showed the expected reception area and anticipated audience levels for a radio station anchored off the Essex coast. Ronan O'Rahilly used a copy of these documents to approach likely backers and eventually managed to raise more than £250,000 of capital from English, Irish and Swiss sources to start his own project, using the name Planet Productions Ltd.

Once funding had been arranged Ronan O'Rahilly engaged shipbrokers to find a suitable ship to house his radio station and eventually an ex-Danish passenger ferry, *Fredericia* was located in Rotterdam. However, the ship's Danish owners, DFDS Ferries, became suspicious that the ship was to be used as a base for an offshore radio station and, being aware of Denmark's anti-offshore broadcasting laws they insisted on including clauses in the sales contract prohibiting the vessel's use for such a purpose.

Negotiations were temporarily discontinued while another broking company was engaged to purchase the vessel and, to avoid any similar setbacks a cover story was devised that the ship would be used to transport cattle from Ireland to England. Despite some misgivings on the part of the brokers about using an ex-passenger ferry for animal transportation, the deal was concluded satisfactorily.

The *Fredericia* sailed from Rotterdam on 13th February 1964 heading for Greenore in Ireland, the port owned by O'Rahilly's father. Because of the O'Rahilly family's control over the port work to equip the vessel for her new role could be carried out there in great secrecy.

At the same time Ronan O'Rahilly was purchasing the *Fredericia*, the Project Atlanta ship *Mi Amigo* was in El Ferrol, Spain undergoing strengthening repairs but Allan Crawford did not have a port to which he could take the vessel to fit her with a new transmitter mast. As part of the 'co-operation' agreement between the two organisations he suggested that if the *Mi Amigo* could be fitted out at Greenore (alongside the *Fredericia*) then Project Atlanta would allow O'Rahilly to use its London studios to pre-record programmes and also provide technical 'experts' to assist with the fitting out of the *Fredericia.*

The deal was agreed and the *Mi Amigo* eventually arrived in Greenore in mid March 1964. The *Fredericia,* which by now had been renamed *Caroline,* was already in the small Irish port being fitted out with broadcasting equipment, including a 168' aerial mast and two 10Kw transmitters.

The name 'Caroline' was reputedly chosen for the ship and the radio station it housed whilst Ronan O'Rahilly was reading a magazine during a flight to America to purchase transmitting equipment.

Like so many of his generation O'Rahilly had been captivated by the charismatic figure of John F Kennedy as he rose through the political ranks to become President of the United States. The fact that Kennedy also happened to be of Irish descent added a further dimension to the cultural empathy felt for him by the young O'Rahilly. Kennedy, with his charm, energy and young family had won the hearts and minds of a whole generation in America and throughout the world. When he was assassinated in Dallas in November 1963 the world was stunned and united in sharing the grief of his bereaved family.

It was a photograph in *Time-Life* magazine of Kennedy's young daughter, Caroline, interrupting a meeting of Presidential advisers at the White House which encapsulated just the right spirit Ronan O'Rahilly wanted for his radio station - a combination of youth, vibrancy and lack of regard for the 'establishment' way of doing things.

The installation of radio and other equipment on board the MV *Caroline* was progressing well, under the supervision of a former BBC engineer, Arthur Carrington, who had pioneered aerial and undersea television transmissions and also been involved in radar research and development for the Government. Although the Greenore port's workforce kept secret the real reason for the ship's conversion it was not long before the town's residents noticed the huge aerial mast

growing to its 168' height and the local newspaper sent a reporter to investigate the mystery ship.

With natural Irish charm the O'Rahilly family circulated a story that the ship was a marine research vessel and needed the tall mast to help it search for deep sea sponges! Satisfied that he had obtained an explanation for the unusual work the reporter left Greenore and his paper printed the story.

So convincing was this cover story that there was little further speculation about the true nature of the activity surrounding *Caroline* or of her future role. The later arrival of the *Mi Amigo*, to have a similar tall mast installed, consequently raised few enquiries from local residents or the media.

Other activities, in particular enquiries made of potential advertisers, did however, lead to rumours and speculation about the planned offshore station. At the beginning of February 1964, the Postmaster General, Reginald Bevins, was asked in the House of Commons about the Government's attitude towards the rumoured plans for an offshore station off the British coast. His reply outlined for the first time the arguments that successive governments would put forward over the next few years against offshore broadcasters:-

"Such broadcasting would contravene international regulations and endanger international agreements on the sharing of radio frequencies. It would almost certainly cause serious interference to radio communications in this and other countries. The Council of Europe has under consideration a Convention aimed at preventing broadcasting from ships on the high seas. This may point to the need for new legislation in due course. Meanwhile I am glad to say that I have very encouraging indications that responsible interests in this country have no intention of supporting any such venture. I am keeping a close watch on the problem."

With both radio ships being fitted out in the same port it was not surprising to hear stories of delaying tactics being employed by each side against the rival station. At one stage the Project Atlanta crew were ordered to anchor the *Mi Amigo* outside Greenore harbour for a few days, which meant no work was done on the ship whilst *Caroline* received the undivided attention of the port's workforce. Also, throughout those few days at anchor the *Mi Amigo* had to ride out a severe storm during which she very nearly ran aground.

In retaliation Project Atlanta recommended to the Caroline organisation some radio technicians who were totally inexperienced and their inept installation of equipment on the MV *Caroline* resulted in severe interference being caused to television broadcasts over a large part of Ireland during a half hour test transmission made from the ship while she was still in port.

A ' boarding party' was subsequently sent by Caroline to the *Mi Amigo* resulting in the disappearance of two Spotmaster tape machines from the Atlanta ship. Needless to say these useful items of equipment subsequently reappeared aboard the MV *Caroline.* Years later both Ronan O'Rahilly and Allan Crawford were able to talk light-heartedly about the 'skulduggery' that had gone on between the two rival groups, but at the time it was all carried out with a very serious objective - to be the first British offshore radio station on the air.

Eventually conversion and installation work was completed on the MV *Caroline* and she set sail from Greenore in the early evening of 23rd March 1964. It was then that Allan Crawford fully realised the Caroline station was not destined to serve the north of England, Scotland and Ireland, but instead it was to snatch his own lucrative target area of London and the south east.

Caroline anchored briefly off the Isle of Man to ride out a storm before sailing south through the Irish Sea, giving her destination as Spain. However, two days later, when the vessel reached Lands End and

changed course entering the English Channel, coastguards all along the south coast of England began to take even greater interest in her, repeatedly asking the Captain for his destination. Captain Baeker, in command of the vessel at the time, would only reply that he was sailing under sealed orders from the owners and refused to reveal any destination.

The authorities were so concerned by the mystery ship that for a short while *Caroline* was shadowed by a Royal Navy destroyer from Plymouth as she sailed through the Channel. By 7.00pm on Good Friday, 27th March 1964 *Caroline* had reached her destination and she dropped anchor three and a half miles off Harwich on the Essex coast.

The first test transmissions took place at about 11.55pm that evening and continued throughout the following morning. Then, at 12 noon on Easter Saturday, 28th March, Radio Caroline officially started broadcasting. The opening announcement was made by Simon Dee: -

"This is Radio Caroline on 199m your all day music station. We are on the air every day from 6.00 in the morning until 6.00 at night. The time right now is one minute past 12, which means it's time for Christopher Moore."

Following this live announcement the opening programme (which was pre-recorded on tape) was a rudimentary Top 20 show, hosted by

The original Radio Caroline ship, MV *Caroline*, later home to Radio Caroline North

Christopher Moore, with the first record being "Not Fade Away" by the Rolling Stones.

On land Ronan O'Rahilly had made preparations for a press conference in London, where it was planned that reporters from all national newspapers and press agencies would witness the start of broadcasts from Radio Caroline. As noon approached, however, O'Rahilly was becoming increasingly anxious about the whole credibility of his project because the radio he had with him in the press conference was only making a series of crackling noises. In desperation he picked it up and beckoned the reporters to follow him outside. They were just in time to hear, with amazing clarity, the opening announcement by Simon Dee. It later transpired that the construction of the hotel chosen for the press conference had the effect of completely blocking out incoming radio signals.

Those on board the MV *Caroline* were uncertain about official reaction to the new station. Initially it was far from clear how the authorities would respond and the biggest concern to the Radio Caroline staff was that the ship would be forcibly boarded and seized whilst at sea. When the time had finally come to put the new station on the air DJs, Simon Dee and Chris Moore on board the MV *Caroline* experienced a sense of uncertainty about what they were doing - daring eachother to actually flick the switch and make the live opening announcement. For the first few

weeks there was a nervous atmosphere amongst the crew and DJs, who lived with the constant fear that at any time they could be arrested, taken back to land and prosecuted for illegal broadcasting.

They need not have worried too much - within four days of the Easter Saturday opening thousands of letters were received at the station's London office and over 300 others arrived at the shipping agent's address in Harwich. As well as letters and record requests the DJs were sent gifts of sweets, cigarettes, chocolates and clothes by enthusiastic listeners wishing to provide them with some home comforts during their long stay at sea.

During the early months of Radio Caroline's transmissions the station's programmes consisted of DJs announcements and, of course, music all day - which was the great novelty and attraction for listeners. Many (but not all) of the early programmes were from the pre-recorded stock which had been made by Simon Dee, Chris Moore and Carl Conway in London studios while the station was still in the planning stage. Tapes were often broadcast more than once and after a few weeks on the air Simon Dee and Chris Moore resorted to editing the recordings by cutting and splicing tapes to vary the order of records!

Listening to recordings of those first Radio Caroline programmes 40 years later, it is hard to believe that the station took off with such immense and immediate popularity. At first, because many of the early programmes were pre-recorded, the DJs only announced record titles and artist's names. As more live programmes were introduced some informal banter did begin to develop, together with comments about what was happening on and around the ship.

The programme content in those very early days was not in any way a structured format, but rather a general blend of pop music by artists such as The Beatles and Cliff

Radio Caroline programme schedule April 1964

6.00am	**The Early Show**	
	(pop and easy listening), Simon Dee/Tom Lodge	
9.00am	**On the Air**	
	(pop, jazz, folk), Carl Conway	
11.00am	**Top Deck**	
	(pop and light ballads), Chris Moore/Jerry Leighton	
12noon	**Music Around Lunchtime**	
	(pop and light ballads), Chris Moore/Tom Lodge	
2.00pm	**Soundtrack**	
	(music from the films), Simon Dee	
4.00pm	**The Big Line-Up**	
	(current pop), Chris Moore/Tom Lodge	
6.00pm	**Downbeat**	
	(jazz, rhythm and blues)	
10.00pm	**Closedown**	
12midnight	**The Late Late Show**	
	(pop, folk, jazz)	
3.00am	**Closedown**	

Richard, mixed with established 'middle of the road' material from performers such as Ray Conniff, Mantovani and Frank Sinatra and new artists such as The Animals and Georgie Fame (both managed at the time by Ronan O'Rahilly).

Even though many of the early programmes were pre-recorded and contained music which was not pop or chart material, audiences in their millions, young and old alike, loved the informality of the station and most of all the unique phenomenon of music being available all day, every day.

In response to growing audience demand Radio Caroline soon increased its airtime from the initial twelve hours a day and continued broadcasting until 10.00pm each night. This was subsequently modified to 8.00pm because of poor night time reception caused by interference from continental stations. Later Radio Caroline started to reopen again on Saturday and Sunday mornings at five minutes past midnight (when the continental stations had closed) and stayed on the air until 3.00am with late night party music.

A Gallup poll published in April 1964, after the station had been on the air for just one month, revealed that out of a potential audience of 20 million listeners aged 17 and above an estimated 7 million had tuned to Radio Caroline's broadcasts at one time or another. What is really astounding about the achievement of such a high audience figure is that, unlike today's sophisticated marketing and promotion of any new product or service, Radio Caroline arrived unannounced, in fact veiled in great secrecy. Even after transmissions had started the station did not promote itself in any other medium (press or poster advertising for example), relying solely on self-generated 'news value' publicity and word of mouth recommendation. This immediate and overwhelming popularity

demonstrated the public demand which existed at that time for an all-day music station, a demand which the established broadcasters had singularly failed to understand or appreciate, let alone tried to provide.

By-mid May 1964, after six weeks on the air, Radio Caroline had firmly established itself with listeners and a growing number of advertisers. The station had also succeeded in demonstrating beyond doubt that there was a substantial demand for the music service and informal style of programming it broadcast.

Following its official opening Radio Caroline had received enormous publicity in the press and on television news bulletins and as word quickly spread about the new all-day music station audience figures grew rapidly.

The station was not popular with everybody however and after just two days on the air complaints were received about Radio Caroline causing interference to communications with lightships and the lifeboat service.

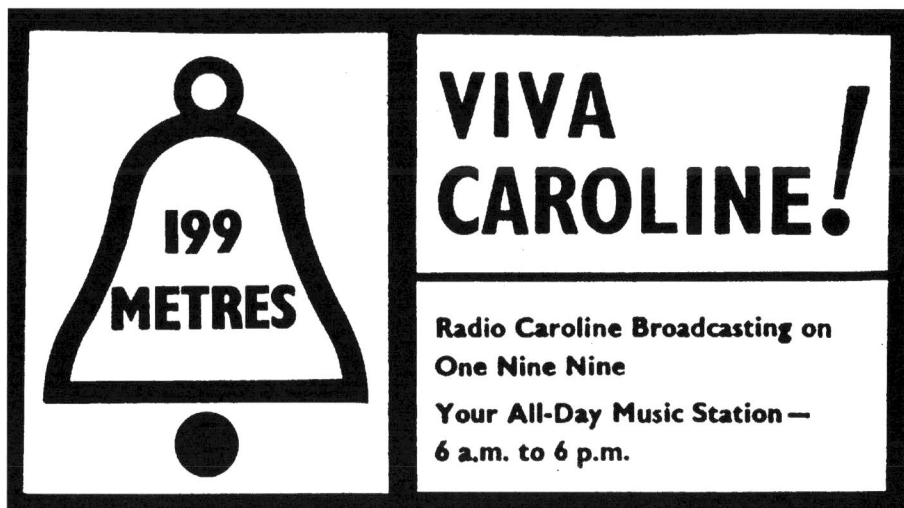

199 METRES

VIVA CAROLINE!

Radio Caroline Broadcasting on One Nine Nine

Your All-Day Music Station — 6 a.m. to 6 p.m.

Hostile reaction to Radio Caroline's broadcasts also came almost immediately in the House of Commons. Questions were raised about Radio Caroline because of fears its signal would affect the emergency services' transmissions, some other MPs, however, spoke of more sinister matters including the dangers of subversive propaganda or publicity for obscene material being broadcast by the offshore station. Postmaster General, Reginald Bevins, promised "action soon" to deal with this and any other offshore radio station which may start broadcasting.

On 1st April 1964 the General Post Office asked the International Telecommunications Union (ITU) to help stop the unauthorised broadcasts. Two days later the ITU replied that it would request Panama, under whose flag the radio ship was registered, to investigate the situation. Meanwhile, radio-telephone ship-to-shore facilities were withdrawn by the Post Office, cutting the station off from direct contact with its landbased offices.

By 7th April the Panamanian authorities were reported to have withdrawn the MV *Caroline's* official registration and on the same day Reginald Bevins told the House of Commons that a number of actions were being planned by the Government against Radio Caroline, including if necessary jamming the station's signal. He also assured the House that the respective record and music industry associations were co-operating with the Government in taking action against the station and that British advertisers had agreed to boycott Radio Caroline.

Meanwhile various authorities made life as difficult as possible for those operating Radio Caroline (and subsequent offshore radio stations). Crew and supplies travelling to and from the radio ship were required to undergo Customs clearance and inspections by water, immigration, Trinity House, port health authorities, the Board of Trade and local harbour authorities.

Although the possibility of jamming Radio Caroline's signal was subsequently dismissed by the Government as an unacceptable option, direct action against the ship at that time could have seen early closure of the station and probably would have frightened off any other proposed offshore broadcasters. The Danish authorities' forcible boarding of the Radio Mercur ship *Lucky Star* in August 1962 had already had just that effect on some of Project Atlanta's original financial backers.

Such direct action against the MV *Caroline* nearly took place on 6th May 1964 when the Royal Navy vessel HMS *Venturous* came alongside and requested permission to board the ship to inspect her bonded stores.

Permission was refused by the Captain of the *Caroline* on the basis that it was a foreign-registered ship anchored in international

waters. As a gesture of goodwill he did offer to allow one man aboard, but this offer was refused by the Customs officials who had come out with the Royal Navy. Listeners to Radio Caroline were kept fully informed of the incident when DJ Simon Dee interrupted normal programmes to explain what was going on and eventually the *Venturous* sailed away without having succeeded in putting a man on board.

Outside of the Government various organisations and authorities also made threatening noises against Radio Caroline (and other offshore broadcasters). In April 1964 Phonographic Performances Ltd. (who collect copyright fees for any public performances of their members' recorded works) threatened to issue a writ against Radio Caroline to prevent the station 'stealing' copyright material. Although nothing definite came of this threat, Radio Caroline, and some later stations, did offer to pay copyright fees, placing Phonographic Performances in a difficult position. On the one hand the organisation vociferously criticised offshore radio stations for not paying fees, but at the same time it did not want to be seen to accept monies from what, in its opinion, were illegal business activities.

In another case of dual standards, major record companies adopted both a public and a private stance towards the offshore broadcasters. Publicly they refused to co-operate with the stations, but behind the scenes all companies, or their representatives, made great efforts to ensure that copies of the latest releases were made available for the offshore DJs to play.

The question of just how the offshore stations impacted on record sales was a controversial one and an argument which lasted throughout the lifetime of the stations. Statistics show that in the first six months of 1965 sales of singles declined by 23% - which record companies attributed directly to the offshore stations. Bill Townsey, a spokesman for Decca Records said:-

> *'People are not buying [records] because of over exposure on the 'pirates'. A record has been played on one station as often as 14 times a day. Being in international waters the pirates needn't pay us a penny and we have no control over what they play.'*

On the other hand the offshore stations opened up the market for smaller record companies - the reason Radio Caroline had been conceived in the first place - and this undoubtedly irritated the larger companies who hitherto had a cartel arrangement in place and were effectively able to control the airplay on Radio Luxembourg.

The impact of the offshore stations in encouraging the launch and growth of smaller record labels can be demonstrated by the fact that in 1961 EMI and Decca accounted for 84% of all Top Ten singles records produced in Britain, but by 1966 their market share had dropped to 57%.

station were beginning to loose their inhibitions about buying airtime.

The very first commercial on the station, aired on 1st May, was for Woburn Abbey, a stately home opened to the public by its owner, the Duke of Bedford. Increased attendances were reported by the Duke in the days immediately after transmission of this commercial and soon afterwards other advertisers also began booking airtime. Amongst early Radio Caroline advertisers were national clients such as Harp Larger, *News of the World,* William Hill's Turf Accountants, Ecko Radios, Bulgarian Holidays, Peter Evans Eating Houses and Kraft Dairylea Cheese.

⚡ I WANT MY CAROLINE ⚡

The Musicians Union too vetoed any of its members taking part in live recording sessions for offshore radio programmes and, despite some early television appearances by offshore DJs such as Simon Dee and Tony Blackburn, entertainment unions and the BBC also later refused to allow such personal appearances on television or BBC radio.

Other media organisations provided a mixed response to the arrival of the offshore radio stations off the British coast. Popular national newspapers were, in general, favourably disposed to the stations - the *News of the World, Daily Sketch* and *The People* bought advertising time as soon as Radio Caroline started broadcasting commercials. The quality press, however, were less supportive with both *The Times* and *The Guardian* publishing a number of articles condemning the activities of the offshore broadcasters.

Advertisers in general were at first reluctant to buy airtime on Radio Caroline, preferring to wait and see what the station sounded like, the size of its audience and more importantly, what, if any, official action would be taken against it or anyone who was seen to be supporting it commercially.

By the end of April 1964, however, advertisers had recognised the huge size of Radio Caroline's audience and in the apparent absence of any official action against the

The biggest boost of commercial confidence for the fledgling station came on 13th May when, in that single day, bookings for £30,000 worth of advertising were received. This surge of interest followed a written statement to the House of Commons the previous day by Postmaster General Reginald Bevins indicating that, although Radio Caroline had allegedly been responsible for interference to British and Belgian maritime communications during its first few days on the air, interference since then had been negligible. He also stated that, for the time being at least, the Government had put off taking any unilateral action against the offshore broadcasters pending the formulation of a concerted approach by all European countries because any British law could be evaded if parallel provisions were not in place elsewhere.

"World in Action" Granada TV

At the beginning of May 1964 Granada Television screened the first British documentary about offshore radio in its weekly current affairs programme, "World in Action".

The programme dealt with the success of Radio Caroline since its launch at the end of March 1964 and featured interviews with the station's founder, Ronan O'Rahilly who, together with Jocelyn Stevens, Chris Moore (Programme Director) and Ian Ross (Sales Director) were filmed in the offices of *Queen* magazine, the original Caroline headquarters.

The then Postmaster General, Reginald Bevins (Conservative) and opposition spokesman Roy Mason (Labour) also appeared in the programme presenting their respective cases. Reginald Bevins stated, not for the first or last time, that the Government was waiting for the Council of Europe to take action internationally before deciding to introduce any domestic legislation to outlaw the offshore radio stations. However, claimed Mr. Bevins, the Post Office had put its point of view about offshore radio to the advertising industry as far back as November 1963 and he was sure that, as a result, the stations would not be able to sell any commercial airtime which they needed to do in order to survive for any length of time.

For the opposition Roy Mason warned that the Government was storing up trouble for itself by delaying to take any action against the stations and stated that there was a threat that the offshore broadcasters would start promoting products which were not permitted to be advertised on British television.

Exclusive footage of the Radio Atlanta vessel *Mi Amigo* being fitted out in the small Irish port of Greenore and of its voyage south around the coast of Britain (including having to put into Falmouth with a storm damaged mast) was featured in the programme as were shots of Radio Atlanta programmes being recorded in a 'secret' London studio. Radio Atlanta's founder, Allan Crawford, was also interviewed about his station and talked of the rivalry with Radio Caroline.

The programme included extracts from cinema films featuring replica 17th Century pirate ships, conjuring up the imagery which was to stay for ever with the offshore stations. It ended with speculation (strongly rebutted by Jocelyn Stevens) that the stations, and in particular Radio Caroline, were financed by a sinister European-based 'Mr. Big', who had vague and undisclosed plans for the future of British broadcasting.

Offshore popularity helps to sell!

The popularity of the offshore stations was often used by radio manufacturers, and others, to sell their own merchandise.

These advertisements all appeared in national newspapers during the 1960's

Meanwhile, as Radio Caroline had been establishing itself off the Essex coast, back in Greenore the Project Atlanta ship, *Mi Amigo,* was still being fitted out with her new aerial mast. By the middle of April 1964 this had been completed and the ship left port on 17th, giving her destination as Spain. The *Mi Amigo* sailed through the Irish Sea, keeping outside territorial waters, but as she approached Lands End the 168' mast began to sway dangerously, seriously affecting the ship's steering. There was nothing the Captain could do but enter British territorial waters to find a calm anchorage off Falmouth while the damage was repaired. However, a Force 8 gale blew up and the *Mi Amigo* was forced to enter Falmouth harbour.

The Captain tried to send a message to Project Atlanta's London office asking for riggers to come to Falmouth and undertake the essential repairs, but Lands End Radio refused to handle the message and it had to be transmitted via a continental station. The riggers were eventually brought to Falmouth to carry out repairs and the *Mi Amigo* set sail again after two days, although the ship received no official attention during her enforced stay in the port.

By 27th April the *Mi Amigo* had arrived at her destination and anchored in international waters off Frinton-on-Sea on the Essex coast, approximately 14 miles from the MV *Caroline,* but three days of rough weather prevented radio technicians getting aboard the ship to arrange test transmissions.

The Radio Atlanta ship, *Mi Amigo*, later home to Radio Caroline South

Radio Atlanta was eventually able to start test transmissions on 9th May and scheduled programmes started three days later on a frequency which was a mere whisker away from Radio Caroline's. It is certain that many people actually heard Radio Atlanta's early broadcasts whilst intending to tune their radios to Caroline.

The station's opening day was punctuated with "Good Luck" messages from contemporary pop stars such as Frank Ifield, Cliff Richard and the Shadows, Harry Seacombe and Rolf Harris. Allan Crawford launched his long awaited station, which had been almost four years in the planning, at a press

---

RADIO ATLANTA

REQUIRE THE FOLLOWING STAFF

Sales Executives: Media selling experience a distinct advantage. Must, however, be conversant with functions of advertising media. Advertising agency experience useful.

Traffic Controller: To manage various procedures surrounding scheduling of airtime bookings. Must have experience. Chance for a frustrated number two.

Sales Co-ordinator: To deal with enquiries (telephone and letter) and generally to liase **(female)** with media department of advertising agencies. A sort of "Girl Friday."

Secretary (1): This position calls for a person conversant with advertising procedures. Ideal type is probably at present employed in media or an advertising agency. Initiative and down to earth common sense essential.

Secretary (2): A personality conscious publicity girl with experience of Public Relations, who can use initiative and who needs little supervision.

Copy Typists: Must be accurate. Work involves contracts, invoices and programme airtime schedules.

Salaries for all above positions subject to negotiation.

All applications addressed to:
LESLIE T. PARISH, PROJECT ATLANTA LTD., 47 Dean St., W.1. Telephone : REGent 7451

conference held in London's Waldorf Hotel. Radio Atlanta initially broadcast for 12 hours a day, but this was quickly extended to 14 hours in line with Caroline's similar extension in late May 1964.

Radio Atlanta's programmes were taped on land for later broadcast from the *Mi Amigo* and although presentation was slicker than the initial Radio Caroline programmes (which were also largely pre-recorded) they lacked the spontaneity of live broadcasting which by mid-May filled almost all of Caroline's daily output. This spontaneity and informality was one major feature of offshore broadcasting which appealed to audiences. The DJs talking about life on board the ship, weather conditions, passing shipping and other snippets of information made listeners feel they were sharing in part of the station's day-to-day life.

As well as presentation style the format of Radio Atlanta also differed significantly from Radio Caroline's. The station programmed different music styles in individual time segments throughout the day - Rhythm and Blues, Latin American, Film Music etc. This contrasted with the general mix played all day by Radio Caroline, whose programme changes (usually every two or three hours) were really only a change of DJ or announcer.

With the history of close links between Radio Caroline and Radio Atlanta and the fact that they were both targeting the same audience in the south and east of England it is not surprising that by early June 1964 rumours began to circulate about a merger between the two rivals. At that time Radio Caroline had been on the air for two months and Radio Atlanta for just three weeks, but it took nearly another month of negotiations before the directors of both stations agreed to a formal merger and a joint press release was issued on 2nd July. The original Radio Caroline ship, MV *Caroline*, was to sail north to the Isle of Man, while the Radio Atlanta ship, *Mi Amigo*, would remain off the Essex coast, but now broadcast under the national call-sign, Radio Caroline.

Without any ceremony Radio Atlanta ceased broadcasting from the *Mi Amigo* at 8.00pm that same evening. After Radio Caroline had also closed for the day, the MV *Caroline* sailed to within a mile of the former Atlanta vessel. The intention was that at 6.00am the following morning it should not be obvious to Radio Caroline's listeners that, overnight, the station had completely

---

Radio Atlanta programme schedule
May 1964

Monday-Friday

6.00am	**Early Call** - Bob Scott
6.15am	**Country and Western Style**-Johnnie Jackson
6.45am	**Early Call** - Bob Scott
7.30am	**Breakfast Club** - Ted King
8.45am	**Musical Mailbag** - Richard Harris
10.00am	**Work Along** - Clive Burrell
11.15am	**Morning Star** - Tony Withers
11.30am	**Spin Around** - Clive Burrell
1.00pm	**Headline Hits** - Tony Withers
2.00pm	**Music the Wide World Over** - Richard Harris
4.00pm	**Sounds of the Sixties** - Tony Withers
6.00pm	**All Systems Go** - Mike Raven
6.30pm	**Music of the Moment** - Neil Spence
8.00pm	**Closedown**

Saturday

6.00am	as Monday-Friday
10.00am	**Downbeat** - Tony Withers
12noon	**Sweet and Lively** - Clive Burrell
1.00pm	**The Saturday Show** - Tony Withers
4.00pm	**Latin Americana** - Clive Burrell
4.30pm	**Best of the Ballads** - Richard Harris
5.00pm	**Country and Western Style**-Johnnie Jackson
6.00pm	**All Systems Go** - Mike Raven
7.00pm	**Music of the Moment** - Neil Spence
8.00pm	**Closedown**

Sunday

6.00am	**Sunrise Serenade** - Richard Harris
8.00am	**Croissants and Cafe** - Clive Burrell
10.00am	**Quality Street** - Richard Harris
11.30am	**Turntable 64** - Tony Withers
2.00pm	**Music the Wide World Over** - Richard Harris
4.00pm	**All Systems Go** - Mike Raven
5.00pm	**Traffic Jam Sessions** - John Ridley
6.00pm	**Nice'n'Easy** - Clive Burell
8.00pm	**Closedown**

transferred operations to what had formerly been a rival radio ship.

Because Radio Atlanta's programmes were mostly taped on land the *Mi Amigo* had no DJ crew and no on-board record library, although there were turntables and a microphone in the studio which had been used in the days of the Scandinavian station, Radio Nord. In order to retain some programme continuity and familiar voices for Radio Caroline's listeners in London and the south east, DJs Simon Dee and Doug Kerr, together with a small supply of records and tapes, were taken across to the *Mi Amigo* to prepare for the next days broadcasting under the new call sign, Radio Caroline South.

ATLANTA NOW CAROLINE - AND CAROLINE LEAVES

RADIO Atlanta , off Frinton ,becomes Caroline this morning. And Radio Caroline is leaving her moorings off Harwich to take up a new position off the Isle of Man.

Once on board the *Mi Amigo* the Radio Caroline staff met some slight resistance from the Dutch Captain who, because of language differences had not fully understood the merger arrangements and anyway did not welcome the prospect of having English DJs on board his ship. He had been happy with the Radio Atlanta arrangement, where the only on-board personnel were the Dutch crew and some radio technicians.

In an effort to thwart the new arrangements the Captain hid vital parts of studio equipment, including styluses for the turntable pick-up arms. Without these the Caroline DJs could not play their records and the planned live programmes of Caroline South from the *Mi Amigo* would be impossible. It was only after hours of persuasion, and eventually by

getting the Captain drunk, that the DJs were able to elicit from him where the missing components had been hidden. By the time everything had been found it was 2.00am and, with essential wiring work taking about four hours to complete Radio Caroline South only just made it on air as scheduled.

Meanwhile, the original Radio Caroline ship MV *Caroline,* after having transferred two of her DJs and a supply of records to the *Mi Amigo* remained at anchor near the former Radio Atlanta ship for most of the day. She eventually set sail in the early afternoon of 4th July, heading for a new anchorage in the Irish Sea. The ship kept outside territorial waters and the DJs who had remained on board, Tom Lodge, Jerry Leighton and Alan Turner broadcast normal programmes during the voyage through the English Channel and northwards up the Irish Sea.

The Captain, Abrahan Hengeveld regularly came on the air to keep listeners up to date with the ship's progress and announce approximate times of arrival off specific coastal towns. The *Caroline* created a lot of interest, with listeners flashing their car headlights at the ship from various vantage points and a local boat owner in Cornwall even took a supply of newspapers out to the ship as she sailed past Padstow.

By 8.00am on Monday 6th July the MV *Caroline* had reached Anglesey off the North Wales coast. She then moved to a position off Dublin for a few days before finally heading to what was to be her anchorage position for almost four years - Ramsey Bay off the northern coast of the Isle of Man. From this position the station, now using the call sign Radio Caroline North, could reach the north and Midlands of England, most of Wales, south west Scotland and much of the north and east of Ireland.

With the two sister stations Radio Caroline was now able to offer audiences and

The Beat Fleet

advertisers what was, in theory, a national daytime commercial radio station. However, the North and South stations each broadcast their own independent programmes and developed quite separate identities. Radio Caroline North broadcast on the original Caroline wavelength of 197m, while Caroline South retained the former Radio Atlanta wavelength of 201m. However, nationally the wavelength of both stations was announced on air as "Caroline on 199m".

Although the outlook appeared promising for the new 'national' offshore station some unexpected problems arose after the merger. Several Atlanta DJs refused to join the new Caroline network and Radio Atlanta General Manager, Leslie Parrish, resigned over a difference of opinion on policy matters.

On Caroline South, over which Allan Crawford retained control, DJs were continually being instructed to play his record company's cover versions of hit singles - as had been the policy on Radio Atlanta. These included, for example, such titles as "Please Please Me" by the Bell Boys and "Needles and Pins" by Tony Steven, rather than the more popular chart hits by The Beatles and The Searchers. This policy caused resentment from the former Radio Caroline DJs, who had previously experienced freedom of choice over which music they played, and this undoubtedly had a detrimental effect on the programming output of Caroline South.

Meanwhile, Radio Caroline North, under Ronan O'Rahilly's direct control, programmed very differently and was able to reflect more accurately audience demand for the new, vibrant beat music, emanating largely from groups based in Liverpool and the north west of England.

As well as programming differences the crewing of the two radio ships also caused unexpected friction after the merger. Originally the *Caroline* had been crewed by the Dutch Wijsmuller Supply and Tendering Company, under the command of one of their captains, Captain Bakker. Once the MV *Caroline* had anchored in position off the Essex coast at the end of March Ronan O'Rahilly engaged his own Captain and crew and Captain Bakker was taken, under cover of darkness, in a wooden rowing boat to Clacton

beach and left to make his own way to his next command. This unusual way of relieving a Captain of his command was due to the fact that the radio ship could not enter British territorial waters because by then Radio Caroline was on the air! After the merger Wijsmuller, which had supplied the Captain and crew for the former Radio Atlanta ship *Mi Amigo,* insisted on also providing a Captain and full compliment of crew for the *Caroline.*

With two stations on the air the Radio Caroline organisation had to also set about solving some practical and logistic problems to supply both ships, to engage sufficient on-air and technical staff, to sell commercial airtime nationally and locally and to deal with the vast number of letters and enquiries from listeners.

Shortly after the merger Radio Caroline moved its administrative headquarters from the *Queen* magazine building in Fetter Lane to a large three storey building at 6 Chesterfield Gardens - renamed Caroline House - in the heart of London's Mayfair. Here, housed on separate floors of this excessively spacious, but most impressive building, were the station's advertising sales team, the administration offices, press and public relations staff and the listener enquiries and promotions department. Studio facilities were also built in the basement to record commercials and promotions for later transmission from the two ships.

Vox Pop

One year we went on holiday outside the area covered by Radio Caroline. I missed the programmes and my favourite DJs very much and couldn't wait to get home (although the holiday was good!).

During the two weeks we had been away many of the DJs had left and when I tuned in again there were a lot of new voices. I felt I had lost some friends without saying goodbye.
John (Ipswich, Suffolk)

The Post Office installed telephone facilities in Caroline House, but refused to list the station by name in the London directory. Not until the end of November 1964 did they reluctantly agree to a listing, but then only as "Caroline Sales". Although the Post Office could not bring itself to acknowledge the existence of Radio Caroline by listing its number in the directory they earned substantial revenue from telephone traffic to and from Caroline House - estimated to be over 2,000 calls each day, an average of one every 15 seconds.

In order to deal with the vast number of enquiries from listeners for information about the station and for items of publicity material such as badges and car stickers, the Caroline Club had been launched shortly before the merger with Radio Atlanta. For 10/6d (55p) listeners could join the Club and in return received an information booklet about the ship and the DJs, a pin badge, car sticker and details of various promotional offers - Caroline T- shirts, fashion accessories etc. After the merger with Atlanta, the Caroline Club was extended to offer membership to listeners on a nationwide basis. The first "Caroline Club Requests" programme was aired on Radio Caroline South on 11th July 1964.

Because of the volume of mail generated as a result of the huge national audience, as well as increased interest from advertisers and the logistical problems of supplying and staffing two ships, Radio Caroline soon opened a second office in Liverpool, to service the needs of the northern station. A northern sales team was also established to sell airtime to 'local' advertisers in the reception area of Caroline North. Listeners to Radio Caroline North were also invited to send record requests and mail for the DJs direct to a Post Office Box address in the Isle of Man, from where it could be taken out to the ship on the weekly tender.

Not everyone was happy though. The arrival of the MV *Caroline* off the Isle of Man with her powerful 20Kw transmitter upset the Island's recently opened (legal) local commercial radio station, Manx Radio. This station, then broadcasting only on VHF (FM) with a power of just 50 watts, complained to the Post Office about interference to its transmissions allegedly caused by Caroline North's powerful medium wave transmitter.

Manx Radio was Britain's first licensed commercial radio station and had started experimental broadcasts, in June 1964 as the result of a prolonged pressure campaign by local businessmen on the Isle of Man, which enjoys a certain amount of independence from the British Government in the conduct of its internal affairs.

In 1959 the Island's Parliament, Tynwald, had authorised the establishment of a 100Kw medium wave radio transmitter on the Isle of Man to boost the local economy and tourist trade and to provide a base for advertisers wishing to reach a large audience on the British mainland. However, a licence from the British Postmaster General was required before any such radio station could be established. Not surprisingly the British Government refused to licence a high power medium wave transmitter because the service would have been a competitor for the BBC, but did, somewhat reluctantly, offer to licence a local station, provided its signal was transmitted on such a low power that it could not be heard on the mainland.

This proposition for a low powered station was not thought to be commercially viable at the time and nothing more happened for nearly five years until two local businessmen, together

---

Radio Caroline North programme schedule July 1964

6.00am	**The Early Show -** Tom Lodge
9.00am	**The Sound of Music** Part 1 -Tom Lodge
10.00am	**The Sound of Music** Part 2 - Jerry Leighton
11.00am	**Top Deck** - Jerry Leighton
12noon	**Date with Caroline -** Alan Turner
1.00pm	**Spinaround -** Tom Lodge
2.00pm	**Soundtrack -** Jerry Leighton
4.00pm	**The Big Line Up** - Tom Lodge
6.00pm	**Sunset Spin -** Alan Turner
9.00pm	**Closedown**
12.05am	**The Late Late Show -** Alan Turner
3.00am	**Closedown**

with the communications conglomerate Pye, formed a new company - the Isle of Man Broadcasting Co - to establish and operate a local commercial radio station on the Island.

In May 1964 the British Postmaster General issued a temporary licence to the new company authorising it to make experimental broadcasts on VHF (FM) only, from a temporary studio housed in a caravan. The first broadcast, under the call sign Manx Radio, took place on 5th June and consisted of a commentary on the world famous TT motorcycle races.

Experimental transmissions by the new local station - four hours a day of music programmes - then continued throughout the summer of 1964. However, the signal was only effectively covering about half the Island and the number of listeners then owning radio sets capable of receiving VHF (FM) broadcasts was estimated at just 2,500. The new local station complained about the frequency and power limitations allocated to them in the light of Radio Caroline's arrival off the Island and eventually, in October the Post Office issued Manx Radio with a further licence to broadcast on 188m in the medium wave band using a power of just 50 watts.

Despite this initial opposition Radio Caroline North soon became accepted by the Isle of Man Government and the Manx people in general. Constant on-air references by DJs to the "wonderful" or "beautiful" Isle of Man together with, at one stage, free promotions for the Manx Tourist Board undoubtedly boosted the Island's tourism figures for the three and a half years the station was anchored in Ramsey Bay.

The Island and its people did not forget this when, in 1967, the British Government tried to impose legislation on the Manx statute book outlawing Radio Caroline and this led to a bitter constitutional dispute.

During the spring and early summer of 1964 while Radio Caroline and Radio Atlanta had been establishing themselves independently and then merging to form an almost national station another development was taking place in the Thames Estuary which, although relatively low key at first, was later to be of considerable significance for British offshore radio. This was the use of semi-derelict wartime defence structures which had been abandoned by the Government during the late 1950s.

In May 1964 David Sutch, an outrageously extrovert pop singer, better known as Screaming 'Lord' Sutch, decided to establish his own offshore radio station. He had been inspired by the success of Radios Caroline and Atlanta, but his station was largely to be a publicity and promotional exercise for himself and other, then unknown, artists.

Sutch had been a rock and roll singer for many years, touring dance halls and gaining notoriety through his outrageous stage act. He first achieved national fame in 1963 when he stood as the National Teenage Party candidate in the Parliamentary by-election at Stratford-upon-Avon. The by-election was attracting an unusual amount of national interest because it had been brought about through the resignation of War Minister, John Profumo, who had been involved in a sex/spy scandal which rocked and ultimately brought down the Conservative Government.

David Sutch failed to win the parliamentary seat at Stratford and lost his deposit, but went on to become a national folk-hero and earn an entry in the *Guinness Book of Records* for standing as a candidate in over 33 parliamentary by-elections as well as a number of general election contests, representing first the National Teenage Party and later the Monster Raving Loony Party.

Together with his manager, Reg Calvert, Sutch hired a small fishing vessel, the *Cornucopia* on which they placed a very low power transmitter, some basic studio equipment and formed an aerial by stringing a wire between the ship's two masts.

Following a press conference and photo session on 24th May 1964 at which Reg Calvert assured sceptical pressmen that this was not a publicity hoax for Sutch and his group, "The Savages" the *Cornucopia* left the Pool of London, supposedly to anchor outside territorial waters and begin broadcasting.

The announced plan was for the station - Radio Sutch - to transmit music daily between 12 noon and 2.00pm and 5.00pm and 8.00pm. There was also talk of late night transmissions being planned, with readings from what were then considered to be risque books such as *Fanny Hill* and *Lady Chatterley's Lover*.

Some broadcasts were apparently made from the *Cornucopia*, when it was not being used for fishing, but when the ship's insurers announced that the vessel was not covered for use as a radio station, David Sutch and his colleagues had to find an alternative base. Their attention turned to the abandoned World War Two sea forts in the Thames Estuary and in particular the Shivering Sands Fort. The radio equipment was transferred from the *Cornucopia* to the Fort, and test transmissions from this new base started on 27th May.

Shivering Sands Fort was a complex of Towers rising from the sea-bed which had been built as part of the nation's coastal defence system during World War Two. The

The Shivering Sands Army fort in the Thames Estuary, used by Radio Sutch and later by Radio City

forts, of which there were originally eight in the Thames Estuary, had been maintained by the Ministry of Defence for some time after the end of the War and were finally abandoned in 1956. One fort at The Nore had been demolished in 1958 as it was considered a hazard to shipping.

The War Office immediately issued a statement saying that Sutch and his crew were trespassing on Government property and that officials, with police support, would go out to the Shivering Sands and instruct them to

leave. A 'boarding party', consisting of an Army Department land agent and a Kent police officer, was sent out to Shivering Sands the following day, but was recalled to Gravesend before reaching the Fort.

In an explanation of the apparent change of policy the Army Department said that it had originally intended to serve a trespass notice on the occupants and to carry out an inspection for any damage to the Fort and the navigational lights housed there. In the meantime, however, the Port of London Authority advised that there had been no damage and accordingly the Army Department representative was recalled.

At the beginning of June 1964 the Minister of State for the Army told the House of Commons in a written reply:-

Although the Fort is no longer required for defence purposes and has remained unmanned for some years it still belongs to the Crown and the persons who took up residence in it last week were, and so far as I know, still are, trespassing.

I understand that they have caused no damage to the Fort, and I concluded last week that immediate action to remove them from what must be a rather uncomfortable spot would not be worth the time and effort involved.

No permission has been given for these people to enter the Fort or to use it for any purpose. The grant of a licence to operate a radio station from a place lying within territorial jurisdiction, as this Fort does, is a matter for the Postmaster General, with whom I am in touch.

The Minister's statement clearly indicates that, from the outset, the Government accepted that

Shivering Sands was within British territorial waters - a factor which was to become the cause of endless confusion and controversy some two years later.

Promoted as "Britain's First Teenage Radio Station" broadcasting hours for Radio Sutch, although advertised as 12 noon - 2.00pm and 5.00pm - 11.00pm, were erratic, with DJs oversleeping and consequently sometimes opening transmissions up to an hour late.

Another reason for the sporadic broadcasts was that, initially at least, the station's transmitter was battery powered and had to be turned off while new batteries were connected or flat ones recharged. Eventually however, the Fort's original wartime generator was repaired and put into working order, but none of the equipment used by the station was of professional broadcast standard and the poor sound quality and weak transmission signal reflected these deficiencies.

Musically Radio Sutch's output favoured rock and roll, rhythm and blues and country and western artists. During the daytime singles and EP (extended play) records predominated, but quite often during the evenings, whole sides of LPs (albums) were played without interruption from a DJ.

Reg Calvert used Radio Sutch to extensively promote the artists and pop groups he managed through a partnership with Terry King and the King Agency. As well as Screaming 'Lord' Sutch and The Savages these included artists such as The Fortunes, Johnny Kidd and the Pirates, Cliff Bennett and the Rebel Rousers, The Rocking Berries, The Hulabaloos and The Outlaws. Recordings by these groups - often only demos or poor quality tapes which had been recorded live at

It has been estimated that in its early weeks Radio Sutch's broadcasts only reached an area of about 50 miles radius from the Shivering Sands Fort - the lucrative target of London was well outside its transmiter range. Reg Calvert later managed to acquire a more reliable and stronger diesel powered transmitter which he installed on the Fort improving the station's signal sufficiently for it to reach parts of outer London.

Regular audience figures for Radio Sutch were never reliably obtained, but they were generally accepted to be only a few thousand compared to the millions attracted to the station's contemporary offshore competitors, Radio Caroline and Radio Atlanta. The station employed no sales staff, but in order to generate some advertising revenue one of its DJs, Brian Paul, tape recorded advertisements appearing in the local Whitstable newspaper and arranged to play them on the air, but not before he had contacted each advertiser telling them about their free 'plug' and the approximate time of broadcast. A few businesses were sufficiently impressed with the response they received and bought further airtime on the station, giving it a little much needed revenue.

Because of the poor quality of its transmissions and the general lack of organisation Radio Sutch never became an established or professional radio station, nor did it seriously try to do so. It was a 'fun' station run as much for the benefit of those taking part in the broadcasts as for any listeners who may have tuned in and it certainly never posed a competitive commercial threat to either Radio Caroline or Radio Atlanta, both of whom were in an entirely different league.

However, although relatively insignificant as a radio station, the importance of Radio Sutch in the history of offshore broadcasting should not be underestimated for two reasons:-

RADIO SUTCH
Britains First Teenage Radio Station
200 Metres Med. Wave 12 to 2 p.m. — 5 to 11 p.m.
Requests & Tapes to Radio Sutch 7 Denmark Street, London W.C.2.

clubs and dance halls - received a disproportionate amount of airtime on the station compared to established chart-listed artists.

(a) Radio Sutch established the principle that the disused and abandoned wartime forts in the Thames Estuary made readily available and suitable bases for offshore radio stations and it was not long before other, more professionally organised broadcasters took up this pioneering example.

(b) Although at first posing no competitive threat during the summer of 1964, Radio Sutch later developed into a station which did become a serious rival for Radio Caroline and the other ship-borne broadcasters, driving two of those stations into a tragic conflict and eventually jeopardising the whole future of British offshore radio.

programmes such as "The Revival Hour", "The Voice of Prophecy" and "The Wings of Healing". The payments received for transmitting these programmes were estimated to have accounted for about 80% of the station's income at this time and enabled it to stay on the air despite the lack of more conventional commercial advertising.

RADIO CITY
LONDON

7 DENMARK STREET W.C.2 · TEL. TEMPLE BAR 6303/4 & 6332/3

KENT & SUSSEX SALES DIRECTOR

OXFORD STREET · WHITSTABLE   TEL. WHITSTABLE 4060

By September 1964 Screaming 'Lord' Sutch, having been offered a concert tour in Australia and New Zealand, was no longer interested in further involvement with the radio station he had founded some four months earlier. His manager, Reg Calvert, who had been the driving force behind the project anyway, acquired Sutch's financial interest and took over complete responsibility for operating the station, which changed its name to Radio City.

During the first few weeks of September 1964 Reg Calvert's new station changed wavelengths three times but reception of the station was still far from satisfactory. Eventually some surplus Navy transmitting equipment was installed on the Fort and from the end of September Radio City programmes could be heard again with a much stronger signal on 238m. The station was on the air for twelve hours a day and the music policy differed from Radio Sutch in that more pop and chart material was broadcast, but always heavily promoting artists managed by Reg Calvert.

The station also achieved a greater degree of on-air reliability than its predecessor, with a pre-determined and advertised schedule of programmes throughout the day. With the improved signal quality the station's broadcasts even managed to reach significant parts of London. Unfortunately, advertisers were still not attracted to Radio City as they were to the more successful Radio Caroline and the only way Calvert could find to generate income for the station was to broadcast taped American religious

In mid-December 1964 another ex-Royal Navy transmitter was acquired by Radio City and music broadcasts were switched to 290m (announced as 299m) while the original transmitter was used to air the sponsored religious programmes on a separate wavelength of 187m. In this way the station was able to broadcast the financially important sponsored religious programmes without interrupting the normal music output, which appealed to most listeners.

Another broadcaster to occupy one of the disused forts in the Thames Estuary was Radio Invicta. This station was launched by a consortium of three men - Kent fisherman, Tom Pepper, Charles Evans (landlord of the "Oddfellows Arms" at Folkestone) and John Thompson (a journalist who had been involved with the planned, but unsuccessful, offshore project in 1962 using the names the Voice of Slough and GBLN). However, quite soon in the life of the station Tom Pepper tried to exclude his partners from the business and this resulted in some ugly incidents involving threats of violence and damage to property.

Radio Invicta based itself on the Red Sands Fort off Whitstable in the Thames Estuary, a sea fort similar in construction to the one at Shivering Sands already being used by Radio Sutch. The station's broadcasts were aimed at Kent, Essex and London and test transmissions were first reported to have taken place on 3rd June 1964, just a week after Radio Sutch began its fort-based broadcasts. For the next few weeks these tests continued using various wavelengths in the medium waveband, but as with Radio Sutch, the transmitter power was always low and reception was poor.

Regular programmes started on 17th July and broadcasts took place for thirteen hours a day from 5.00am - 6.00pm. Radio Invicta's format had a bias towards middle of the road, easy listening music and proved popular with a dedicated audience in the station's small reception area, because it provided a musical alternative to the pop based offshore stations on the air at that time.

The station was promoted in publicity material as "The Good Music Station" and programmes carried titles such as " Date with Romance", "Memory Lane" (largely using old 78rpm records) and "Pot Luck" - a record request programme in which the listener asked for a specific record number to be played. The number supposedly corresponded to a number in the station's record library, but in fact the on-air DJ played whatever he wanted, whilst keeping up the pretence of the 'lucky number' system.

As with Radio Sutch, Radio Invicta, because of its low power and weak signal, had difficulty attracting advertisers and carried very few commercials. Ironically it was Tom Pepper's desire to obtain more advertising revenue that led to tragedy for him and ultimately spelt the end of the station altogether.

Radio Invicta
programme schedule August 1964

5.00am	Early Morning Spin
7.00am	Breakfast Show
9.00am	Top Sticks
10.00am	Mail Call
11.00am	Strictly for Highbrows
11.30am	Pot Luck
12.55pm	Information Desk
1.00pm	Lunch Box
2.00pm	Date With Romance (Mon-Fri)
	A Seat in the Stalls (Sat & Sun)
3.00pm	Memory Lane
4.00pm	Afternoon Session
4.30pm	Kiddies Corner
5.00pm	Music for the Evening
6.00pm	Closedown

RADIO INVICTA
The Good Music Station
ON 306 METRES

Chapter 4   Competition and Goodguys

By late November 1964 there were four offshore radio stations on the air from bases off the British coast (Radio Caroline North, Radio Caroline South, Radio City and Radio Invicta) while two others (Radio Atlanta and Radio Sutch) had opened and closed during the preceding six months. With such intensive activity it might be thought no more developments would take place before the years' end, but two significant events did happen in those final weeks of 1964 involving the opening of a major new offshore station and the tragic end of another.

On 19th November 1964 the former US Navy minesweeper, *Galaxy*, dropped anchor within sight of the Shivering Sands Fort (home of Radio City) and started test broadcasts using the call sign Radio London. The ship had been fitted out as an offshore radio station in Miami, from where she had sailed three weeks earlier.

The station broadcasting from the *Galaxy* was the brainchild of Don Pierson, a Texas businesman who, in April 1964, had heard about the launch of Radio Caroline, paid a fact-finding visit to Britain to see what offshore radio was all about and, convinced of the commercial profitability of such a venture, returned to the USA to develop his own project.

Radio London was run by a highly professional and well organised team and from the outset it threatened to become a serious challenger to Radio Caroline. The *Galaxy* boasted a 212' aerial mast and a powerful 50Kw transmitter enabling the station to reach most of southern England and the Midlands. Additionally, Radio London's programming and advertising sales teams were far better organised than those of its rivals and the station sounded professional and successful from the start.

Radio London's initial investors included a consortium of Texas businessmen with backgrounds in construction, car dealing and banking. A trust fund, Marine Investment Co. Inc., registered in Grand Bahama, leased the ship from another company, Panavess Inc. of Panama and purchased the broadcasting equipment which was later installed on the vessel in Miami. Advertising sales for Radio London were handled by a British-registered company, Radlon (Sales) Ltd. which operated from offices in Curzon Street, London W1. Altogether total initial investment in the station was estimated to have been over £1.5million.

RADLON (SALES) LTD   17 CURZON STREET LONDON W1   MAYfair 5361
Directors: P. T. Birch (Managing). G. J. W. Bean T.D., F.C.A.

Gordon McLendon (owner of Dallas station KLIF and ex-partner in the Swedish offshore station Radio Nord) acted as programme consultant to the new station while an ex-advertising agency account executive, Philip Birch, was hired as Radio London's Managing Director in England. Advertising professionals, Alan Keen and Dennis Maitland joined the sales department of Radio London from the world of newspaper and magazine publishing.

Because of the contacts Radio London had been able to establish through this experienced sales team the station was able to go on the air with a number of 'blue chip' advertising contracts from day one, adding considerably to its instantly professional sound. The early successes of the sales team continued and during its first year on the air Radio London broadcast commercials for over 250 nationally known brands or products including Beechams medicines, Shell petrol, Players Richmond cigarettes, Carreras Guards cigarettes, various washing powder brands produced by Unilever and national magazines including *Reveille* and *Bride.* Sponsored programmes also came from CEMA Bingo, Currys Electrical shops, Peter Stuyvesant cigarettes, Vernons Pools, Brooke Bond Tea and S and H Pink Trading Stamps.

The Beat Fleet   **27**

Before its launch Radio London had planned to do something no other British offshore station had attempted - provide a regular and comprehensive news service. This plan revealed the influence of the station's American programme consultant Gordon McLendon who had developed the concept at his station in Dallas and successfully introduced a similar service on the former Swedish offshore station, Radio Nord.

A number of news agencies were approached to provide the service but Reuters and Associated Press made it clear from the outset that they were not willing to provide a feed of news to Radio London. Another agency, United Press International did, however, make an offer to provide Radio London with a news service, but the cost was prohibitive and the offshore station decided not to accept the proposal.

A tentative agreement was then reached with the *Sun* newspaper, which in 1964 was published by Odhams Press and was generally considered to be the mouthpiece of the British Labour Party - a very different publication from its present day descendent with the same title. However, having made an initial agreement to supply Radio London with news Odhams's solicitors advised that, because of legal uncertainties about the status of offshore radio stations, the *Sun* should withdraw its offer.

So, having failed to secure a regular supply of news from any of the established sources Radio London had to resort to the professionally unsatisfactory, but convenient and inexpensive arrangement later adopted by all other offshore stations - it pirated news from the bulletins of other broadcasters, mainly the BBC and Voice of America.

Long before the MV *Galaxy* arrived off the

British coast stories of the professionalism and technical superiority of Radio London worried those managing Radio Caroline. It is now known that during the weeks before Radio London came on the air Ronan O'Rahilly, aware of the new station's superior sales expertise, approached Philip Birch suggesting a merger of the two advertising sales organisations - Caroline Sales and Radlon (Sales). From Radio London's point of view this was never taken as a serious proposition, and a response containing a series of demands which were inappropriate and unacceptable to Radio Caroline, quickly put an end to the suggestion.

However, had O'Rahilly's approach succeeded it would have been Radio Caroline which benefited most from the deal because the sale of commercial airtime was one of that station's biggest weaknesses and that defect was destined to cause the organisation some fundamental problems during the following twelve months.

Ronan O'Rahilly continued to monitor preparations being made by Radio London for a launch at the end of 1964. When the *Galaxy* arrived in the Thames Estuary and Radio London started broadcasting from the original anchorage near the Shivering Sands Fort he quickly realised it could be liable to prosecution as it was within British territorial limits. O'Rahilly advised the rival management about possible consequences for all offshore broadcasters if the new station continued broadcasting from inside territorial

Radio London's ship, MV *Galaxy*, at anchor off the Essex coast

waters. This friendly warning was heeded and the *Galaxy* moved to an anchorage off Frinton-on-Sea, Essex, near to the *Mi Amigo,* home of Radio Caroline South, and certainly outside British territorial limits.

Test transmissions from this new position started on 5th December 1964 on 266m but stopped abruptly the following day because problems were being caused by structural features within the MV *Galaxy.* The vessel, being a former minesweeper, was fitted with miles of copper wiring to help in the detection of mines and this was having an adverse effect on the radio transmissions. Engineers had to set about fully insulating the studios and transmitters to prevent further interference to the signal and no further broadcasts were heard from Radio London until 18th December.

Radio London's first programme schedule, December 1964

6.00am	**Pete Brady Breakfast Show**
9.00am	**Earl Richmond Show**
12 noon	**Dave Dennis Show**
3.00pm	**Tony Windsor Show**
6.00pm	**Kenny Everett Show**
7.00pm	**The World Tomorrow** (sponsored religious programme)
7.30pm	**Kenny Everett Show**
9.00pm	**Closedown**

News bulletins were broadcast each hour on the half hour, with weather on the hour.

Apparently now satisfied with the performance of all technical equipment and the strength of its signal Radio London started regular transmissions at 6.00am on 23rd December 1964. The opening announcement was made by Pete Brady:-

'Radio London is now on the air with regular broadcasting. The station will bring to Britain the very best from Radio London's Top 40, along with the up-to-date coverage of news and weather, Radio London promises you the very best in modern radio.'

"I Could Easily Fall in Love" by Cliff Richard was the first record played on Radio London.

Radio London's format was strictly based on the Top 40 (known on the station as the Fab 40) with records being allocated to one of three categories which were played on a rotation basis each hour. Category A were the top ten records of the week, Category B were the remainder of the Top 40 and Category C were new releases. There were also slots in the format rotation for LP tracks and Flashbacks (old Fab 40 hits).

Initially the American backers had wanted to name the station Radio KLIF (London), with tapes of the Dallas station's programmes being rebroadcast in an undiluted American style to an unsuspecting British audience. However, they eventually settled for a change of name to Radio London (Big L), with a watered down version of the highly Americanised Top 40 format, which it was thought would be more acceptable to British listeners.

This fundamental disagreement over format, although patched up at the time of the station's launch in 1964, was to lead quite soon to some of the initial backers withdrawing from the Radio London project to set up their own all-American format offshore radio station.

While Radio London was successfully launching itself as Britain's newest offshore broadcaster another station was experiencing some traumatic and dramatic times.

Early in December 1964 Radio Invicta's owner, Tom Pepper, approached the *News of the World*, which at that time was advertising quite extensively on Radio Caroline, asking the newspaper to consider also buying airtime on his station. The *News of the World* agreed to one trial commercial being broadcast and indicated that, if found to be satisfactory, there was a possibility that it would purchase further airtime on Radio Invicta.

Tom Pepper considered this offer from the country's biggest circulation newspaper to be a major breakthrough for his struggling little station and wanted his Senior Announcer and Programme Director, Ed Moreno, to voice the live commercial. Moreno was off the station on shore leave at the time, but Pepper persuaded him to return to the Red Sands Fort to prepare for the commercial's transmission.

The two men left Faversham harbour in the station's 'tender', the 36' long *David*, early in the morning of 16th December 1964 after experiencing great difficulty starting the small ship's engine. After Ed Moreno, as well as some fresh food supplies, had been transferred to the Fort, DJs Simon Ashley and engineer Martin Shaw joined Pepper for the return journey in the *David* and some welcome Christmas shore leave. They departed from Red Sands shortly after 11.00am and those left behind on the Fort noticed that the *David's* engine again appeared to be spluttering as she disappeared into the mist.

At about 6.00pm the same day a police launch came to the Red Sands Fort and reported that Tom Pepper's body had been found near Reeves Beach, Whitstable, tied to a small wooden life raft. Ed Moreno was asked by the police to leave the Fort and formally identify Pepper's body, but before doing so he hurriedly recorded a tribute to his former boss which was aired on the station the following day. More wreckage and oil drums were later found floating in the sea near the Street Buoy, but of the three men on board the *David* that day only one other body was ever found. Even then it was several months later and had become so badly decomposed that it was only identified from a tape recording of a Radio Invicta programme found in a pocket of the clothing.

In the immediate aftermath of the tragedy Pepper's widow and his former partners Charles Evans and John Thompson continued to operate Radio Invicta, but there were many disagreements about ownership and station policy. There was speculation in the press at the end of 1964 that The Batchelors pop group, whose records were extensively promoted on Radio Invicta, were interested in buying the station, but nothing definite ever came of this story.

As 1965 dawned both Radio Caroline stations were undoubtedly market leaders in offshore commercial radio, but Caroline South's position was about to be seriously challenged by Radio London, which had arrived just before Christmas 1964. Radio City was also starting to establish itself as a minor challenger to both Caroline South and Radio London, but the other fort-based station, Radio Invicta, was going through a crisis following the drowning of its owner and two staff and in February it quietly closed.

Radio Caroline North started the new year with some problems too, this time caused by rough weather on the night of 13th/14th January when the starboard anchor chain snapped. With the other anchor unable to hold in the severe storm, the *Caroline* began to drift, but eventually the Captain manoeuvered the ship so that she remained outside territorial waters and rode out the storm. Within a week a new one and a half ton anchor and four and a half ton chain were installed on board the radio ship.

A Labour Government had been returned in the October 1964 British General Election and consequently a new Postmaster General, Anthony Wedgewood Benn was now in charge of matters relating to offshore radio stations. For the first few months of his period in office he continued his predecessor's procrastination over dealing with the 'problem' of offshore broadcasters, always arguing that there were higher legislative priorities and that concerted action by all European Governments was the way forward.

The first step towards achieving this action came on 22nd January 1965 when member states of the Ministerial Committee of the Council of Europe signed "The European

---

Sir Winston Churchill

Britain's wartime Prime Minister, Sir Winston Churchill, died in January 1965 and in recognition of the significant contribution he had made to the destiny of the nation he was accorded a State Funeral - almost unprecedented for a person who was not a member of the Royal Family.

The State Funeral took place on Saturday 24th January 1965 and while the BBC Radio services carried a commentary and coverage of the service and subsequent tributes the two main offshore radio stations paid their own tribute to the former statesman.

Radio London actually closed during the funeral service, then played classical music and recorded tributes for a large part of the remainder of the day. Radio Caroline also played classical music and broadcast its own documentary detailing the major events of Churchill's life, but unlike Radio London the station remained on the air all day.

Agreement for the Prevention of Broadcasts Transmitted from Stations Outside National Territories" more commonly known as the Strasbourg Convention. Under the terms of this Convention any state which signed or later ratified it agreed to also enact domestic legislation to prohibit the establishment of offshore broadcasting stations and to prevent any collaboration with such stations by their citizens. The Strasbourg Convention applied to any ships, aircraft or other floating or airborne objects under the jurisdiction of a particular country, but importantly it did not go so far as to permit action to be taken directly by one state against ships, aircraft or citizens of another. It was, however, left to individual countries, once they had ratified the Convention, to legislate through their own parliaments to ban offshore stations broadcasting from off their coasts.

Although British legislation did not come before parliament immediately after the signing of the Strasbourg Convention the issue of offshore radio was raised in the House of Commons in March 1965. The Postmaster General was asked for details of instances where interference had been caused to legitimate broadcasters by offshore radio stations. In a written reply he detailed 19 cases where offshore stations had allegedly caused interference to maritime communications and in seven of these Radio Caroline was identified as the culprit, an allegation which was later hotly disputed by the station's management and technical experts.

Despite the moves in European parliamentary circles to start the process of outlawing offshore radio a milestone was reached at Easter 1965 when Radio Caroline celebrated its first birthday. Birthday messages and greetings from over twenty artists were recorded and included in programmes on both the North and South Caroline stations during the Easter weekend. To mark the occasion the station also introduced four 'Bell Awards' which were presented to various artists for their contribution to

musical entertainment during the preceding twelve months. Recipients were -

The Animals - best group record of the year ("House of the Rising Sun")
The Beatles - best and most consistent artists
Petula Clark - best female recording ("Downtown")
Tom Jones - best male recording ("It's not Unusual")

At the end of its first year on the air, Radio Caroline had achieved advertising income of £294,000, with running costs estimated to be between £100,000 and £150,000. This was a significant achievement in the British marketing environment which was largely unfamiliar with the use of radio as an advertising medium. Unfortunately for the station, much of this advertising revenue had been earned during its first nine months, prior to the arrival of the far more professional Radio London in late December 1964.

The impact of the new rival is apparent from the advertising revenue figures for March 1965 which show that Caroline South was struggling to achieve an average income of just £1,000 per week. The growing popularity and professionalism of Radio London contrasted strongly with the weaknesses of Radio Caroline's management structure and commercial airtime sales techniques. These deficiencies were to cause further internal problems at Radio Caroline later in the year.

In the face of the stiff competition from Radio London, Radio Caroline's management decided to revamp the station's tired and out-dated format - something which had never been addressed before. A news service, Caroline Newsbeat, was introduced in April 1965 and in May the Caroline South DJs were

Rate Card No.2
effective from 1st August 1964

Radio Caroline
199 metres medium wave

Caroline South

SPOT ANNOUNCEMENT TARIFF

Programme Times*	Time Class	60	45	30	15	7
6.00 - 7.00 a.m.	C	£50	38	25	15	10
7.00 - 8.30	A	£100	75	50	30	20
8.30 - 12.00	AA	£120	90	60	40	25
12.00 - 3.00 p.m.	A	£100	75	50	30	20
3.00 - 4.30	B	£70	50	35	25	15
4.30 - 9.00	A	£100	75	50	30	20
'ROD' Spots		£30	22	15	10	—

Caroline North

SPOT ANNOUNCEMENT TARIFF

Programme Times*	Time Class	60	45	30	15	7
6.00 - 7.00 a.m.	C	£30	23	15	10	7
7.00 - 8.30	A	£60	45	30	20	15
8.30 - 12.00	AA	£80	60	40	25	17
12.00 - 3.00 p.m.	A	£60	45	30	20	15
3.00 - 4.30	B	£45	35	23	15	10
4.30 - 9.00	A	£60	45	30	20	15
'ROD' Spots		£20	15	10	7	—

*Advertisers may specify the quarter-hour segment within the programme in which the Spot Announcement will be made.

re-launched as personality "Caroline Goodguys", modelled on a similar successful initiative by one of New York's most popular music stations of the mid- sixties, WMCA. But, most importantly, programme content was changed to a format based on the "Sound 65" chart (to rival Radio London's "Fab 40") although this was later changed to the "Caroline Countdown of Sound", a Top 50 chart.

Both Caroline stations also began to broadcast an hour-long programme each evening sponsored by Roulette Records, which was pre-recorded in New York and hosted by the legendary American DJ, Jack Spector (from station WMCA in New York).

This revamp of Radio Caroline's format resulted in increased interest from audiences and advertisers. An indication of the dramatic decline in Radio Caroline's advertising revenue after the arrival of Radio London in December 1964 and of a revitalisation after the format changes in April 1965 can be seen from these monthly advertising income figures:-

November/December 1964 £47,952
(before Radio London arrived)

December1964/January 1965 £28,721
(after Radio London's launch)

April/May 1965 - £49,259
(after the revamp of Radio Caroline's format)

Unfortunately this sudden transformation in style and format - effectively an Americanisation of the station, diluted for the benefit of British listeners - did not come across to the audience in quite the way it was intended. The Caroline DJs, or "Goodguys" were uncomfortable with their new image and many of the sponsored programmes on the station at that time conflicted both in content and presentational style with the hurriedly introduced psuedo-American format.

The simple reason for this was that during late 1964, before Radio London's launch, Caroline had succeeded in selling a large number of 15 and 30 minute sponsored shows which were produced directly by advertising agencies on behalf of their clients. The sponsors included significant national 'blue chip' brands such as Player's Anchor cigarettes, Andrews Liver Salts, Princes Foods, Chappell Pianos, Fynon

Liver Salts and Miners Make-up, giving the station an aura of respectability as well as much needed revenue.

Many of the contracts were for daily or weekly segments to be broadcast over periods of 13 or 26 weeks - well into 1965 and long after the station's format change. The problem was that nearly all these sponsored programmes were hosted by well known 'establishment' personalities such as Anne Shelton, Kenneth Horne, Stirling Moss and Vera Lynn, who were more likely to have been heard at the time on the staid and dated BBC Light Programme than a vibrant, youthful offshore radio station with an adapted American format.

Radio Caroline itself had little or no direct input into either the musical content or presentation of these sponsored segments and when they were inserted into the station's own revitalised live programming the two styles inevitably clashed. Although very lucrative for Radio Caroline these programmes were probably responsible, in the south at least, for large numbers of listeners retuning their radios to a rival station, particularly Radio London, and a radio audience, once lost, is notoriously difficult to recapture.

Despite its perceived success everything was not immediately perfect at Radio London either. To the average listener the station sounded far more professional and, more importantly, in touch with their current musical tastes than any of the other offshore broadcasters. However, during the station's first few weeks on the air many of the DJs struggled with the presentation of Radio London's American style Top 40 format. Nevertheless Radio London still came across as a more listenable station, particularly in comparison to Radio Caroline South, which in the early months of 1965 was suffering from an identity crisis due to a lack of a clearly defined programme format.

Following the demise of Radio Invicta in February 1965 two of Tom Pepper's previous partners, Charles Evans and John Thompson, together with DJ Mike Raven and a group of other Kent businessmen decided to take over what was left of the station. Although some of the backers soon withdrew from the new project Mike Raven decided to go ahead with the plan and, together with two colleagues, took some new studio equipment out to Red Sands Fort in March. The Fort's transmitter was soon returned to working order and test transmissions began for a new station, KING Radio.

After about two weeks of testing regular programmes for KING Radio started on 24th March 1965. The format was deliberately designed to be different from all the other offshore stations then on the air. Keeping away from the pop music Top 40 format, KING Radio played middle-of-the-road, country and western, rhythm and blues and Latin American music together with a sprinkling of pop classics. DJs often read short poems or greeting card verses between records and for a time the station promoted itself with the slogan "Wonderful Words - Wonderful Artists".

KING Radio had its landbased offices in Folkestone, Kent and the station's signal reached the south east coast, part of East Anglia and even outer London. Unfortunately the format never really caught the imagination of listeners, nor did it attract the support of many advertisers, achieving audience figures of only about 20,000 at peak listening times.

After KING Radio had been on the air for a few months it became apparent to financial backers that, in its existing state, the station would never be commercially successful. One of these backers, David Lye, although concerned about the financial viability of

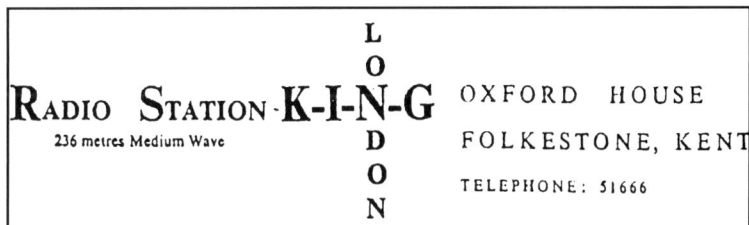

RADIO STATION·K-I-N-G LONDON
236 metres Medium Wave
OXFORD HOUSE
FOLKESTONE, KENT
TELEPHONE: 51666

KING Radio, was still convinced that a non-Top 40 format station could be successful if it were properly structured. With this view firmly in mind he approached a business colleague, public relations consultant Ted Allbeury, to see if he could produce any ideas for improving the station's image and ratings.

Ted Allbeury, as well as being a public relations consultant was also a farmer and later became a successful author of spy thrillers, many based on his own wartime experiences in the Intelligence Corps. A report from his consultancy, Allbeury Coombes and Partners, was presented to the owners of KING Radio suggesting the introduction of a radically different format for the ailing station, one which relied totally on what they referred to as 'sweet music' presented as an audio magazine targeted at a specific daytime audience sector - housewives.

As well as a general format the actual style of presentation was also addressed in the report and it was recommended that the brash, psuedo-American approach adopted at the time by other offshore stations should

KING Radio programme schedule

7.00am	**Rise and Shine**
8.00am	**Mike and Mandy's Breakfast Show**
9.00am	**Country Style**
9.30am	**South of the Border**
	(Latin American) -weekdays
	All That Jazz (Saturday)
	Concert Hall (Sunday)
10.00am	**Mailbeat** (Dedications)
11.00am	**Music from the Shows**
11.30am	**Our Kinda Folk** (Folk Music)
12 noon	**Lunchbox**
2.00pm	**Melody Hour**
3.00pm	**Memory Lane**
3.30pm	**Lucky Numbers**
4.30pm	**Stateside 65**
5.00pm	**Up and Coming** (new releases)
6.00pm	**Raven Around** (Rhythm and Blues)
7.00pm	**Closedown**

be avoided by the proposed new easy listening station in favour of a strictly 'British' style.

In summary the report recommended that the programmes should be "sweet in flavour and soft in presentation". A further important recommendation was that the range of the station's transmissions should be increased to cover the most important market areas, namely London and the whole of the south east of England, rather than just the Kent and Essex coast and outer London then being covered by KING Radio.

At first it was planned to rename the station Radio Eve, but Ted Allbeury quickly realised that this title reflected only the target audience and did not convey the station's wavelength to

by Allbeury Coombes and Partners was used to raise new financial backing and a new company, Estuary Radio Ltd., was formed to operate the revamped station.

Eventually fresh capital was raised and Ted Allbeury was appointed Managing Director of the new station, with full responsibility for implementing the whole scheme. Much of the new capital was used to buy out the previous owners of KING Radio and to purchase new technical equipment in line with the objective of substantially increasing the station's coverage area. A new 10Kw transmitter was purchased and installed on Red Sands Fort during the summer of 1965 and at the same time a 200' aerial mast was erected on one of the towers.

Red Sands Fort, home to Radio Invicta and later Radio 390

Inside another of the towers two air conditioned studios were custom-built, to a design used at that time by the New Zealand Broadcasting Corporation. Each studio had two turntables, a microphone, seven-channel audio console, two tape decks and cartridge players for commercials. Power for broadcasting requirements and the living quarters was developed from two of the Fort's original wartime generators which were re-commissioned, together with new ones installed in another of the towers.

potential listeners. As the wavelength would not necessarily be published in the press or appear on radio dials, a decision was made to change the station's name to Radio 390. The concept of an audio version of a women's magazine was retained, however, under the umbrella title "Eve-The Woman's Magazine of the Air" and daytime programme content was to be directed mainly at the 'housewife' audience.

On adoption of these recommendations by the owners of KING Radio, it quickly became obvious that new capital would have to be injected into the station before the plans could be implemented. The business plan prepared

While these improvement works were taking place on Red Sands Fort KING Radio continued to broadcast, but that station finally closed on 22nd September 1965. Its transmitter did, however, remain on the air for a further few days broadcasting a taped announcement asking listeners to re-tune to Radio 390.

Radio 390 made its first test transmissions on 23rd September 1965 with regular programmes of easy listening or 'sweet' music, starting a few days later. The first record played on the new 'sweet music' station, which broadcast for eighteen hours a day, was "Moonlight Serenade" by Glenn Miller. The term 'sweet music' as interpreted by Radio 390 in fact included a wide mix of non-pop music, ranging from 'standards' of the 1930s and 1940s, through jazz, rhythm and blues, military and organ music, to contemporary light music.

There were no DJs on Radio 390, presenters were known as 'announcers' and were positively discouraged from promoting themselves as personalities, then a common practice on the Top 40 format stations. In keeping with its overall policy of projecting a 'respectable and traditional' image the station also adopted the practice of closing its transmissions at the end of each day by playing the National Anthem.

A number of other programming innovations were also adopted by Radio 390 - a daily programme for pre-school children, "Playtime" and a five minute 'radio cartoon', "Moonmice", both of which started immediately after BBC Radio's "Listen With Mother" children's programme had ended at 2.00pm. Another 'first' for offshore radio was the daily soap opera "Dr. Paul", which Radio 390 bought in from Australian commercial radio and aired at the same time each day as the BBC's soap "Mrs. Dale's Diary". Ted Allbeury also later started his own Sunday evening 'fireside chat' programme under the title "Red Sands Rendezvous" in which he talked to listeners about a wide range of topical issues.

Unlike its predecessors on Red Sands Fort (Radio Invicta and KING Radio) Radio 390 was an immediate success with audiences and advertisers alike. From the outset the station attracted advertising contracts from large and well-known national advertisers - the first commercial it transmitted was for the national weekly magazine, *Reveille*. Ted Allbeury's imaginative concept of targeting a different audience from the other offshore stations and playing a completely different type of music proved that there was indeed a place in the market for an easy listening station.

Radio 390's success was also assisted by the strength and quality of its transmission signal. The combined aerial and Fort tower height of 290' enabled the station to use a wavelength which was a

---

Radio 390 programme schedule (Weekdays)

6.30am	**Bright and Early**
7.00am	**Morning Melody**
7.50am	**Revive Your Heart**
8.00am	**Morning Melody**
9.00am	**Stars on Disc**
9.30am	**Light and Bright**
10.15am	**Masters of the Organ**
10.35am	**Pause for Prayer**
10.45am	**Keyboard Cavalcade**
11.00am	**LP Special**
11.15am	**Dr. Paul** (Australian soap)
11.30am	**Music From the Shows**
12 noon	**Lunchbreak**
1.00pm	**From Me to You**
2.00pm	**Playtime** (children's programme)
2.10pm	**Moonmice** (children's programme)
2.15pm	**Melody Fair**
3.15pm	**Spotlight**
3.30pm	**Intermezzo**
4.00pm	**Memory Lane**
4.30pm	**Tea Time Tunes**
5.00pm	**Music Bound**
6.00pm	**Scene at Six**
6.30pm	**The World Tomorrow** (sponsored American religious programme)
7.00pm	**Country Style**
7.30pm	**From Me To You**
8.00pm	**Dinner at Eight**
8.30pm	**Continental Cabaret**
9.00pm	**Serenade**
11.55pm	**Thoughts at Midnight**
12 midnight	**Closedown**

News bulletins were broadcast at 9.00am, 1.00pm, 5.00pm and 9.00pm daily

---

clear channel away from the more crowded middle and upper end of the medium waveband. This combination of clear wavelength and aerial height enabled the station to cover a large area including most of south and south-east England, East Anglia, the Midlands and a large part of Wales, certainly far in excess of the management's initial expectations.

The power put into the transmitter was usually only 10Kw, but a maximum of 35Kw was sometimes achieved by the station's engineers. Ironically, a listenership survey carried out by the BBC in October 1965 estimated that Radio 390 must be using a power of at least 60Kw, such was the strength of the station's signal throughout much of the south east of England.

Over on Shivering Sands Fort Radio City was fast becoming a significant rival in the battle for offshore radio audiences. Whilst not achieving the level of advertising income of either Radio Caroline South or Radio London, it was nevertheless earning over £20,000 a month, mainly from sponsored American religious programmes. With running costs of only £2,500 a month Radio City claimed to be so successful financially that its owner Reg Calvert explored the possibility of opening a second fort-based service, using another of the abandoned Thames Estuary Forts -Knock John.

Equipment was landed on Knock John Fort by Radio City staff who proposed to start test broadcasts for a new station during the summer of 1965. Unfortunately for Radio City another potential offshore radio operator, Essex businessman Roy Bates, already had his sights set on the Knock John Fort and a bitter, sometimes violent, territorial dispute broke out between the two rival groups.

Reg Calvert made a further attempt to launch a second station in April 1965 when he tried to purchase an ex-supply boat from the Royal Navy. He planned to anchor this vessel in the Bristol Channel and use it as a base from which to beam radio and possibly television programmes, to the west of England, Wales

Caroline Continental

During the summer of 1965 Radio Caroline South started broadcasting a programme aimed at its many thousands of listeners in Europe. "Caroline Continental" was broadcast each Sunday morning between 10.00am and 11.00am and consisted of record dedications to and from listeners in Germany, France, Holland and Belgium as well as Britain. The programme was hosted by Garry Kemp who spoke seven foreign languages.

A commercial opportunity was also exploited by this programme, promoted as a service to British advertisers who wanted to sell their products in Europe, which at that time was not a single market as it is now. Under the title 'Radio Caroline Export Drive' British advertisers were offered up to an 80% discount on standard rates, and commercials were produced in up to four languages.

and the south Midlands. However, the project did not materialise and with the loss of Knock John Fort to Roy Bates's group the idea of Radio City launching a second station was shelved for the time being.

Attention was turned instead to improving coverage for Radio City itself. In June 1965 professional riggers erected a new 240' aerial mast on Shivering Sands Fort, a new 10Kw transmitter was installed and broadcasting was extended to thirteen hours a day.

Radio City must be credited with introducing some truly innovative programmes into its schedule.

As well as the usual DJ shows, the station aired a daily request programme - The 5 x 4 Show - with only Rolling Stones and Beatles records being played.

The Auntie Mabel Hour, devised and hosted by Ian McRae, was a satirical comedy lampooning just about every aspect of 60's pop culture. This included offshore radio

RADIO CITY CLUB
299 metres

itself when a spoof broadcast by 'Radio 310' (based on easy-listening station Radio 390) was included in one programme. The Auntie Mabel Hour also presented a special pantomime edition on Christmas Day 1966, with all DJs on the station taking part.

The Anti-City Show was an opportunity for listeners to send (on tape) their criticisms of the station and its programmes. These were broadcast un-edited as a true example of customer feedback.

In addition Reg Calvert regularly arranged for recordings to be made of live concerts he promoted in Kent and Essex, featuring artists he managed, and for these to be broadcast on Radio City.

In August 1965 Radio Caroline South increased its hours of transmission with the introduction of the "Party Time" programme from 9.00pm-12 midnight on Fridays and Saturdays. Also about this time a new shift pattern was introduced for the DJs, giving them two weeks on the ship, but only one week ashore instead of two as had previously been the practice.

This change in shift rota coincided with the sudden departure (either because they were fired or had resigned) of a number of the early Radio Caroline DJs including Doug Kerr, Garry Kemp, Jon Sydney, Mike Allen and Roger Gale. These departures, ostensibly over the revised working arrangements, revealed a deeper problem facing Radio Caroline and in particular Caroline South at the time. An

internal inquiry had criticised many of the DJs for sounding unenthusiastic about the new 'Goodguys' format, arguing that they lacked the commitment to compete effectively with the much more vibrant Radio London.

A Gallup poll in the autumn of 1965, the results of which were not published at the time, showed that in its primary target area Caroline South had only a 0.9% audience share compared to Radio London's 14.7% and the BBC Light Programme's 30.4%. The poll also revealed that the largest daily audience for Radio London was between 11.00am and 1.00pm (780,000), while for Caroline South it was between 5.00pm and 7.00pm (160,000).

As a consequence of the listening pattern revealed by these figures Radio Caroline's advertising income fell dramatically during 1965. Radio London was picking up all the lucrative commercial contracts and the bulk of the Caroline network's revenue was coming as the result of national campaigns, which included the coverage area of Caroline North. In effect Caroline North was subsidising the operation of its sister station and had Caroline South been a single operation rather than part of a national network it is doubtful whether, commercially, it would have survived after 1965.

By contrast Caroline North was highly successful at this time and in fact throughout its entire life. There are a number of reasons for this, but Radio Caroline North held a unique monopoly position and although other stations were planned to compete for northern

audiences none ever materialised. Caroline North experienced some minor competition in 1966, but only on the fringe of its coverage area, from Radio Scotland (particularly while that station was anchored off the west coast of Scotland and off Northern Ireland) and Radio 270 (anchored off Yorkshire). However, neither of these smaller stations made any dramatic impact into Caroline North's primary area and the station always attracted a large and dedicated audience not only in the north of England, but in Wales, Scotland, Northern Ireland and along the east coast of Southern Ireland.

The programme output from Caroline North was always far more suited to its audience than that of Caroline South. Ronan O'Rahilly maintained direct control over Caroline North after the merger with Radio Atlanta and gave DJs the freedom to play the music they knew listeners wanted to hear. Geographically, too, the station covered an area of the country which in the mid-1960's was the home of pop music - Liverpool and north west England. It is hardly surprising therefore that the DJs were able to relate closely to what their audiences wanted to hear and the station's programming reflected this close contact.

Caroline North also benefited from a talented team of DJs and in particular the first Programme Director, Tom Lodge, who was responsible for deciding the station's programming style. Tom Lodge had a background in US radio and knew from personal experience how to programme for what listeners wanted to hear on their radios. It is no coincidence that in 1966 Tom Lodge together with another successful Caroline North DJ, Mike Aherne, were brought south to help re-launch Caroline South and build up its audience figures.

Airtime sales - the lifeblood of any commercial radio or television station - were also more successful in the north. Although Caroline North benefited from the large national campaigns, indeed its very existence made that national advertising possible, the station also carried a huge volume of 'local' advertising. This local advertising was sold by a team based in the station's Liverpool offices,

but covered the whole of the north west of England, Wales, Scotland and Ireland and many businesses in these areas soon became household names through advertising on Caroline North. By contrast direct sales for Caroline South by the stations's own staff were only bringing in a few hundred pounds a week by the autumn of 1965 and the Gallup poll report even recommended closing the Chesterfield Gardens Sales Department entirely as it was not considered cost effective.

Another potential offshore radio station operator was interested in the Thames Estuary Forts during 1965. Roy Bates an Essex fisherman and businessman decided to investigate the possibility of starting his own radio station after witnessing the early success of Radio Caroline and the initiative of Screaming 'Lord' Sutch in making use of the abandoned Thames Estuary wartime forts.

Roy Bates spent some months in late 1964 and early 1965 visiting the various forts and selected an ex-Navy fort at Knock John to be the base for his planned station. The ex-Navy Forts, of which there were then four still standing (the other three were Roughs, Sunk Head and Tongue Sands) had been built to an entirely different design from the former Army structures at Red Sands and Shivering Sands. The Navy Forts were much smaller overall and consisted of a single tower with a platform mounted on two concrete legs. Living quarters were built on top of the platform as were the anti-aircraft batteries,

Radio Essex programme schedule

6.00am	Get Up and Go Type Show
9.00am	Good Morning Show
12 noon	Afternoon Spin
3.00pm	The Sound of Music
6.00pm	Big Bands
7.00pm	Essex Goes Pop
8.00pm	An Evening with Essex
11.00pm	Essex Beat Club
3.00am	Night Owl

News bulletins were broadcast on the even hour between 8.00am and 8.00pm except Sundays when it was on the odd hour between 9.00am and 9.00pm. Weather forecasts were aired on the half hour.

while the concrete legs of the Forts were hollow and provided eight storeys of storage areas for ammunition and supplies.

Having identified the Fort he wanted to use for his station, to be known as Radio Essex, Roy Bates set about raising finance, acquiring equipment and finding broadcasting and engineering staff. These arrangements took a few months to complete and during the summer of 1965 when Bates was finally ready to start installing the broadcasting equipment he returned to Knock John to discover that

Knock John Navy Fort in the Thames Estuary - used by Radio Essex

Reg Calvert of Radio City -who had also identified Knock John as a suitable base for his proposed second outlet - had already landed some of his own equipment and staff on the Fort.

The Radio Essex men asserted their 'right' to use Knock John and the violent struggle which ensued between the two rival groups resulted in the Radio City staff being forcibly evicted from the Fort. After this Reg Calvert abandoned plans to launch a second station based at Knock John.

Roy Bates and his group then set about restoring two of the wartime generators to provide power for the Fort and also constructed rudimentary studios in one of the old storerooms. Broadcasting equipment was primitive and consisted of some low power domestic and government surplus items. The

transmitter was a pre Second World War ex-USAF radio beacon which had been converted for broadcasting use. An aerial mast was also constructed on top of the Fort using some scaffolding poles and lengths of copper wire.

Test transmissions from Radio Essex started at the end of October 1965 with regular programmes beginning officially on 7th November. The format consisted of easy listening music during the day and pop based Top 40 music at night.

Radio Essex transmitted on a very low power and its primary coverage area was the county of Essex. It claimed to be mainland Britain's first local radio station, announcing itself as "The Voice of Essex" and to this end concentrated on securing advertising mainly from local companies and businesses.

Initially the station broadcast for fourteen hours a day, but Radio Essex later became Britain's first 24 hour a day radio station, with night-time transmissions attracting a small, but regular audience. The 24 hour schedule continued six days a week with a six hour closedown early on Monday mornings to enable transmitter maintenance work to be carried out.

A more ambitious plan to use a Thames Estuary fort as a broadcasting base was announced in October 1965 by two Essex businessmen, Eric Sullivan and George Short. They formed Vision Productions with plans to launch an offshore radio and television station from the ex-Navy fort at Sunk Head.

Structually Sunk Head was one of the least stable Thames Estuary Forts, having been damaged when it was hit by a ship in the 1950's, but it was taken over by Vision Productions in October 1965 at about the same time Roy Bates was launching Radio Essex. Test transmissions for the proposed radio station - Tower Radio - took place at the end of October, at first on numerous wavelengths until eventually 236m was selected as being most satisfactory. Unfortunately, the very low power of the transmitter and constant technical problems meant that the station's broadcasts could hardly be received on land, except along the immediate Essex coastal area.

Sunk Head Fort, used by Radio Tower

interests. Radio Tower eventually began its programming on 29th April 1966 and continued on very low power for about two weeks, the last reported transmission being on 12th May.

At the beginning of June Peter Jeeves, Joint Managing Director of Vision Productions, the company behind Radio Tower, issued a statement admitting that the station had experienced repeated technical problems in putting out a good signal. Also, apart from one or two shops in Colchester and Clacton, no advertisers had been attracted to the station and as a consequence without sufficient commercial revenue the project had foundered.

Claims were made that test transmissions for Tower TV took place during the early hours of 9th November 1965, with a blurred picture of a test card said to have been received on Channel 5 in Essex. The television station from Sunk Head Fort was in fact a hoax although there were some photographs published which indicated that such a venture may have been planned. In fact the station's owners had been 'warned off' by government officials who indicated that if television transmissions were started action would be taken to seize the Fort and remove anyone who was found to be in occupation.

Test transmissions for Tower Radio did, however, continue throughout November and regular broadcasts were announced to start on 1st January 1966, but the tests ceased abruptly on 20th December and nothing more was heard from the Sunk Head Fort for over three months.

Transmissions began once again at the beginning of March 1966, this time the station was calling itself Radio Tower and test

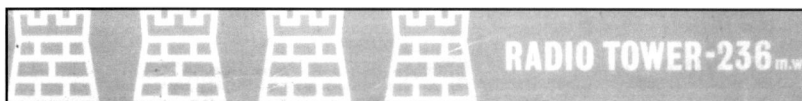

broadcasts took place on a number of wavelengths. Announcements were made that regular programmes would begin shortly and the new station's format was to be directed at a local audience, with news and current affairs programmes as well as features for 'minority'

In September 1965, at the same time Radio 390 was replacing KING Radio the other established fort-based station, Radio City, was negotiating with ship-based rival Radio Caroline about a possible merger.

After losing Knock John Fort (the base for his planned second station) to Roy Bates's Radio Essex group Reg Calvert approached the Project Atlanta side of Radio Caroline, through Major Oliver Smedley, offering Radio City for sale. This approach was supposedly to raise capital for his latest plan - a somewhat improbable project to launch an offshore television station from a submarine on the sea-bed, but the deal did not proceed entirely as planned. Project Atlanta was not as enthusiastic as Calvert about acquiring Radio City, largely because of its own financial difficulties and the serious staffing and format problems facing Radio Caroline South at that time.

However, some initial discussions did take place when it was envisaged that Radio Caroline South could be transferred to the

Shivering Sands Fort, while the *Mi Amigo* would sail either to the north east of England or the Bristol Channel, to provide a third outlet for the Caroline network.

The outcome of these negotiations was an agreement that Project Atlanta would arrange for the installation of a 10Kw transmitter on Shivering Sands Fort which could be used to provide an improved signal when Radio Caroline South transferred there. However, when the equipment was delivered it was found to be 25 years old and in such a poor condition that it failed to work properly.

This transmitter, which Oliver Smedley had obtained second-hand from a radio station in Fort Worth Texas, was later to feature significantly in the battle for control of the offshore airwaves. Because the supposedly 'new' transmitter was useless Radio City had to continue broadcasting with the equipment installed on the Fort nearly twelve months earlier and the plan to transfer Radio Caroline South from the *Mi Amigo* was abandoned.

Despite the setback over the transmitter some other positive agreements did come of the negotiations between Radio City and Radio Caroline South which, although stopping short of a full merger, brought the two stations closer together. These included an amalgamation of the two advertising sales teams and an agreement for Radio City to relay Caroline's "Newsbeat" news service, as well as airing promotions for some Caroline South programmes. In return Project Atlanta was to pay Radio City's tendering, fuel and other day-to-day operating costs. From Radio Caroline's point of view it was hoped that the amalgamation of the two sales teams would help relieve the desperate advertising situation brought about by the strong competition from Radio London which had been starkly highlighted in the recent, but then unpublished, Gallup poll.

The merger of the sales teams came into effect on 1st October 1965, but was not a success. Within three months the arrangement had been terminated by Radio City amidst allegations that it was owed up to £8,000 in advertising revenue and that its tendering and other operating costs had not been paid by Project Atlanta. Radio City took back responsibility for the sale of its own airtime and payment of its operating costs with effect from 1st January 1966, while legal disputes about the money owed from the joint sales operation continued for many months afterwards.

Within the Radio Caroline organisation the financial position of Radio Caroline South (Project Atlanta) had become desperate and in December 1965, following the collapse of the joint sales arrangement with Radio City, Ronan O'Rahilly's Planet Productions acquired its assets and at the same time Allan Crawford resigned from the station's board of directors.

The merger agreement between the two rivals which had been negotiated in June 1964 had, in many respects, been something of a sham. Although to the average listener Radio

---

**Radio City programme schedule
January 1967**

6.00am	**Early Bird Show**
7.30am	**Voice of Prophecy** (American religious programme)
8.00am	**Breakfast Break**
8.30am	**Allen Revival Hour** (American religious programme)
8.45am	**Up and About**
10.00am	**Just Go**
10.45am	**Coffee Break**
11.00am	**Just Go**
12noon	**Gary Stevens Show**
1.00pm	**Breakaway**
5.00pm	**Five by Four**
5.30pm	**Sixty Minute Special**
6.30pm	**Voice of Prophecy** (American religious programme)
7.00pm	**City by Night**
11.00pm	**Late Date**
12midnight	**Closedown**

News and Weather on the hour

Caroline appeared to be a national network the two component stations had been run quite differently, one (Caroline South) under the control of Allan Crawford and the other (Caroline North) under Ronan O'Rahilly's influence. This situation had now been rectified by O'Rahilly gaining complete control of both ships and the radio stations they housed. Despite the elimination of Project Atlanta from the Caroline organisation at this time the Project's Chairman and largest shareholder, Major Oliver Smedley, (who had also been involved in the now failed joint arrangement with Radio City) retained ownership of his 60,000 shares.

With O'Rahilly's Planet Productions now having complete control of both Caroline stations plans were prepared to introduce technical improvements, particularly for Caroline South, to counter the stronger signal of rival Radio London. A wavelength change and substantial increase in power was planned for the *Mi Amigo*, but as so often in the history of offshore radio the forces of nature were to intervene before these ambitious plans could

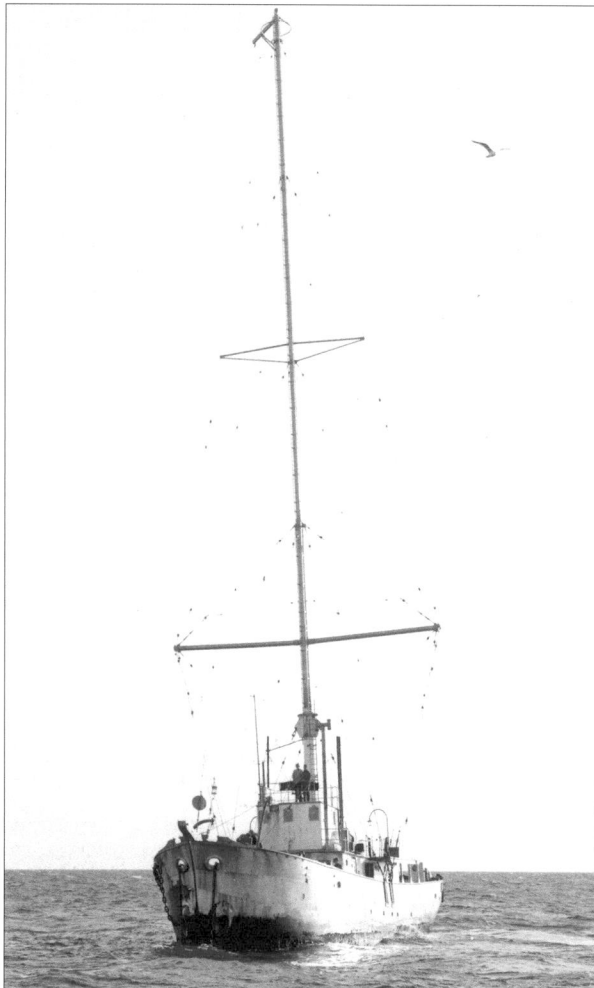

be put into effect and caused the Caroline organisation unexpected problems during the early months of 1966.

Consideration was also given in the autumn of 1965 to ways in which reception of Radio Caroline North could be improved in its target area. One idea was to move the anchorage position of the MV *Caroline* from Ramsey Bay in the Isle of Man to a position nearer the mainland. In order to assess the most suitable location plans were made for the *Caroline* to set sail on 30th October 1965 on a cruise across the Irish Sea to Fleetwood in Lancashire then down the coast across Liverpool Bay and around the North Wales coast ending near Llandudno.

Listeners were invited to fill in reception log forms during the weekend cruise, stating how the quality of the station's signal had varied each hour with the change in the ship's location. Clive Singleton, spokesman for Caroline North was quoted in a press article as stating, "I have been concerned for some time about the number of our listeners who live in pockets [of poor reception]. I feel that we must be able to offer 100% reception throughout the UK. This exercise is a way of finding out if a new location close in to England is the answer. Caroline's move is obviously part of a battle with Radio London to remain Britain's number 1 station." However, the planned cruise never actually went ahead due to bad weather and shortly afterwards plans to relocate the *Caroline* from Ramsey Bay were abandoned.

As 1965 drew to a close yet another offshore radio station was preparing to take to the air.

Back in October 1964 a group of Scottish businessmen had formed a company, City and County Commercial Radio (Scotland) Ltd., which was registered in the Bahamas. Publicly the directors of the company declared that they wanted to apply for local radio licences in various Scottish cities including Glasgow, Edinburgh, Aberdeen and Dundee. However, the real, and rather thinly disguised, reason for the company's formation was to launch an offshore commercial radio station to serve the whole of Scotland. The public face of the company

Radio Scotland's ship, the *Comet*

was Tommy Shields, an ex-employee of magazine, newspaper and comic publishers, D C Thomson and a long-time advocate of commercially funded broadcasting.

During the summer of 1965 Tommy Shields located an ex-Irish lightship, *Comet* which he considered suitable to use as a base for the new offshore station. The *Comet*, which had no engines, had to be towed from Ireland to Guernsey in the Channel Islands where she was stripped of all superstructure and fitted with a 145' aerial mast, two 10Kw transmitters and on-board studio facilities.

Work on the *Comet* was only completed shortly before Christmas 1965 and the radio ship was towed from the Channel Islands towards her proposed anchorage near Dunbar in the Firth of Forth off the East coast of Scotland. However, during the journey the tow line snapped and the problems encountered in securing a replacement line meant that the *Comet* did not finally arrive at her anchorage until the early hours of 30th December, three days later than had been planned. Consequently there was no time for proper test transmissions before the new Scottish station was officially launched shortly before midnight on Hogmanay, 31st December.

Because of this last minute rush to put the station on the air vital items of equipment were still missing and work on fitting out some of the technical facilities had not been completed. Consequently early transmissions caused interference to maritime communications in Scotland, drawing accusations of irresponsibility from the Postmaster General and the Coastguard Service.

Initially the station broadcast for 16 hours a day and the declared programme policy for Radio Scotland was that 60% of output would consist of pop music, with the other 40% being traditional Scottish interest. Radio Scotland took advantage of the recent staff purge at Radio Caroline South by engaging some of its former DJs (notably Roger Gale, who became Radio Scotland's first Programme Director) to help launch the new station.

Radio Scotland, was beset with technical problems and forced to transmit on low power until the middle of January when a vital component arrived from the USA enabling the station to significantly increase its transmitter power. Despite this increase, however, Radio Scotland's signal, whilst good in Edinburgh and along the east coast remained poor on the western side of Scotland, particularly in the commercially important Glasgow area. Radio Scotland's first few weeks on the air with repeated breaks in transmission, a weak signal in the heavily populated west of Scotland and poor quality programming, led to dissatisfaction amongst listeners and resulted in a sharp decline in advertising revenue.

In an effort to attract larger audiences and a greater number of advertisers, the station's programme format was changed substantially from what had originally been envisaged. Radio Scotland abandoned its promised emphasis on Scottish programming and concentrated instead on a Top 50 chart format, with only about 15% of airtime being given over to Scottish programmes such as "Ceilidh" and "Larry Marshall and the One o'Clock Gang". The station also started promoting itself as 'Big S' in imitation of Radio London's 'Big L' slogan.

Radio Scotland's opening programme schedule

11.50pm	**Welcome to Radio Scotland**
11.59pm	**Auld Lang Syne**
12.00	**Ceilidh** with David Kinnaird
2.00am	**Beatles Show '66** (sponsored by the station's first advertiser, the *News of the World*)
2.30am	**Top 50 of '65** with Roger Gale
5.00am	**Scottish Top Twenty**
6.00am	**Rooster Call**
9.00am	**Hit the Deck**
12 noon	**The 242 Clan**
2.00pm	**Popscotch**
3.00pm	**Line Up**
4.00pm	**Blast Off**
7.00pm	**Look Ahead**
7.05pm	**Radio Church of God**
7.35pm	**Interval** (actually the station closed for a few hours because of poor night-time reception)
10.30pm	**Saturday Stampede**
12.30am	**Night Owls**
2.00am	**Closedown**

Throughout the early months of 1966 Radio Scotland continued to experience difficulties in achieving a satisfactory signal to reach the heavily populated west of the country - although it was attracting a mailbag of about 1,000 letters a day from listeners in places as far away as Denmark, Sweden, Norway, Holland, Germany and south east England! Despite this widespread popularity the station's primary target area was Scotland and it was clearly failing to reach large sectors of that potential audience.

In an attempt to solve this problem Radio Scotland's management decided at the end of April 1966 to tow the *Comet* around the north of the country to a new anchorage off the west coast, near the holiday resort of Troon. The station had planned to continue broadcasting throughout the 1,000 mile, month long voyage, but this idea had to be dropped because of technical problems encountered on the *Comet*. When the vessel did eventually arrive off the west coast Radio Scotland was able to provide a much better signal to Glasgow and the west of Scotland.

Despite all its technical and programming difficulties Radio Scotland's presence off the northern coast of Britain had a tremendous impact on those listeners who could receive the broadcasts. For the first time here was a radio station whose output was directed specifically at its Scottish audience and not treating listeners as an afterthought on a 'national' service, which was the case with the predominately London-based radio service from the BBC.

Although for commercial reasons Radio Scotland had been forced to modify its initial pledge on the proportion of Scottish programme material, by doing so the station had in fact helped bring many aspects of the 'Swinging 60's' north of the border. This applied not just to music but the whole ethos of that era. At last young people in Scotland could keep in touch with the changing fashions, tastes and attitudes of those vibrant mid-60's years.

Vox Pop

Up here in Scotland we had heard about Radio Caroline and Radio London, but couldn't pick up their signals. Sometimes at night we could just about hear something of Big L, but that was all.

Then Radio Scotland arrived and we felt 'this is our own pirate'. It was much better than the BBC and played the latest hits all day. At last we had our own radio station for young people.

Iain (Edinburgh)

Chapter 6   Expansion and tragedy

The early weeks of 1966 were stormy off the whole of the east coast of Britain. During the evening of 11th January, in a Force 8 gale, the Radio London ship *Galaxy* began to drag her anchor and drift towards the shore. By the early hours of the following morning the crew had managed to start the *Galaxy's* engines and were able to prevent the ship drifting any further towards land, but by that time she was only two miles from Clacton beach, clearly inside British territorial waters. Because of this transmissions did not start as usual that morning and it was not until the *Galaxy* was towed back to her anchorage in international waters later in the day that Radio London was able to resume broadcasts after seven hours of silence.

A week later, on 19th January the Essex coast was experiencing yet more bad weather with another Force 8 gale and driving snow. At 9.00pm that evening Walton-on-the-Naze coastguards noticed that the Radio Caroline South ship, *Mi Amigo*, was not at her usual

the radio ship and although the message was flashed on television screens during the evening's programmes it was not successful in alerting the crew.

With the crew still oblivious to their own plight, Walton-on-the-Naze lifeboat was launched and the Clacton lifeboat stood by ready to provide assistance if necessary, while Caroline South's own tender, *Offshore One*, left Harwich to try to assist the radio ship. It was only shortly before the tender reached the *Mi Amigo* that the crew realised their perilous situation, but by then it was too late and, as repeated attempts were made to start the engines, the ship drifted further and further towards land.

At around midnight the *Mi Amigo* ran aground at Frinton-on-Sea, narrowly missing one of the many concrete groynes which are situated all along that stretch of beach. The Captain put out a Mayday call requesting assistance, but neither the lifeboat nor *Offshore One* could get close enough in the shallow water off the

---

Pop ship Caroline adrift

Tug Goes To Aid Of Grounded Pop Ship
Eight Taken Off By Breeches Buoy: Six Stay Aboard

---

position and appeared to be dragging her anchor. The swivel rope controlling the ship's three anchors had snapped and, without anyone on board realising, the *Mi Amigo* had begun to drift towards the coast.

Attempts by the coastguard and North Foreland Radio, using emergency channels and even flashing lamps to warn the *Mi Amigo* that she was adrift, were unsuccessful. Radio Caroline's agent in Harwich, Percy Scadden, also tried to alert the crew by flashing his car headlights at the radio ship, again without success. Anglia Television was asked to broadcast a warning message to the crew of

beach to help those on board the stranded radio ship. In freezing temperatures and heavy seas members of the Coastguard Service, together with auxiliaries from the Walton Life-saving Apparatus Company, were able to rig up a Breeches Buoy and, in an operation illuminated only by parachute flares, five DJs, two radio engineers and a steward were taken off the ship. The Captain and six crew members stayed on board the *Mi Amigo* while coastguards and lifeboat crew stood by for what turned out to be a further 36 hours to provide assistance if required. The rescued DJs and radio crew were taken to a hotel in Walton-on-the-Naze where they were given food and dry clothing.

When daylight broke on 20th January it became apparent just how fortunate the *Mi Amigo* had been - a few yards either side of her were those concrete groynes, which if she had struck one it would almost certainly have damaged the radio ship beyond repair. As it was the vessel was listing slightly and had already sunk about four feet into the soft sand on the beach.

The noon high tide gave the *Mi Amigo* a severe buffeting, threatening to drive her further on shore and smash the ship against the sea wall. During the afternoon a Dutch salvage tug took up position some 500 yards offshore and a cable was attached to the *Mi Amigo*. On the midnight high tide numerous attempts were made to drag the stricken radio vessel off the beach, but the re-floating attempt had to be abandoned when the five inch thick tow line snapped under the tremendous strain.

By the time of the next high tide the Captain of the *Mi Amigo* had decided to try and free the vessel himself using an operation known as kedging. This involved attaching the *Mi Amigo's* anchor to a long cable and taking this out into deep water where it was dropped until it held on the sea-bed. Then, by a combination of winching on the cable and using the power of her own engines the *Mi Amigo* successfully pulled herself out of the sand and was re-floated on the incoming tide.

Once free of Frinton Beach the Captain anchored the *Mi Amigo* about a mile offshore while divers inspected her hull. Some minor damage had been sustained by the radio ship and it was decided that before returning to her anchorage she should be taken to Holland for permanent repairs to be undertaken.

Radio Caroline South, beleaguered throughout 1965 by the loss of advertising revenue to Radio London, a series of on-air staff changes, an unsuccessful format change and, most significantly, a general lack of cohesive management, now found itself off the air altogether for what appeared likely to be an indefinite period while the *Mi Amigo* was undergoing repairs.

However, an unexpected helping hand came from Scandinavia, where the last remaining Swedish offshore station, Radio Syd, had itself recently been forced off the air due to

extensive pack ice forming in the Baltic Sea. The station's owner, Britt Wadner, had her ship *Cheeta 2* sail south for safety intending to anchor her in the comparatively warmer waters off the Dutch coast until weather conditions in the Baltic improved. After hearing of what had happened to the *Mi Amigo* she immediately offered to divert the *Cheeta 2* to England to provide a temporary base from which Radio Caroline South could recommence broadcasts. Not surprisingly Ronan O'Rahilly readily accepted the offer.

Cheeta 2 arrived off Harwich just eleven days after the *Mi Amigo* had run aground, but Radio Caroline South's broadcasts could not restart immediately because the Swedish radio ship was only equipped for FM transmissions. Bad weather prevented the necessary modification works being carried out for some days and it was not until the afternoon of 12th February that test transmissions for Radio Caroline South were able to start from the *Cheeta 2*, but they were only on a very low power.

Major Minor Records

In February 1966 Radio Caroline's management company, Planet Productions Ltd. acquired the services (and financial investment capital) of a new full time working director, Philip Soloman, who had previously worked for Decca Records and had been an agent and concert promoter, mainly for Irish groups, including The Batchelors.

One of Philip Soloman's early initiatives was to launch a record label which would be used by Radio Caroline to extensively promote unknown artists. He negotiated deals for the records to be manufactured by CBS under the label Major Minor and for them to be distributed by Selecta Records, a subsidiary of Decca.

Contractual problems delayed the launch of the Major Minor label until November 1966, when both Caroline stations suddenly began to heavily plug its first two releases by relatively unknown Irish groups, the O'Brien Brothers and Odin's People. The lack of success in achieving national British chart ratings for these two releases was hardly surprising, but it led to Major Minor negotiating deals with American record companies to launch already successful material by US artists such as the Isley Brothers and Kim Western on to the UK market.

When regular programmes eventually began transmissions had to be restricted to 10.00am - 4.00pm because reception during the hours of darkness was impossible on such low power, even in nearby Essex and East Anglia. The transmitter on board *Cheeta 2* constantly caused trouble and Caroline South was repeatedly off the air during February and early March. Various items of technical equipment had to be brought from the *Mi Amigo* in Holland and installed on board the *Cheeta 2* to boost her power and eventually the normal broadcasting hours were re-introduced.

Unfortunately for Caroline South more problems followed in late March when the *Cheeta 2* began to take in water after being buffeted for three days by gale force winds and had to be towed into a Lowestoft shipyard for repairs. *Cheeta 2* left Lowestoft in the late evening of 1st April, with broadcasts from Radio Caroline South starting once again the following morning.

Meanwhile, in Holland the *Mi Amigo* had been undergoing repairs and the opportunity was taken by Radio Caroline management to install a new 50Kw transmitter, enabling the station to compete more effectively with the powerful signal of rival Radio London.

On 7th April the *Mi Amigo*, now fully repaired and with new radio equipment on board arrived back off the Essex coast and test transmissions on a new wavelength of 259m started a few days later. However, within a few hours a short in the aerial mast brought these broadcasts to an abrupt halt and bad weather prevented engineers repairing the aerial immediately.

Frustrated by yet more delays adding to the length of time Caroline South had been off the air and knowing that Radio London was about to increase its own transmitter power, Ronan O'Rahilly set out in a tender to try and deal with the problem personally. However, before he arrived one of the station's DJs, Tony Blackburn, managed to climb the *Mi Amigo's* mast and remove the rogue wire which had been causing the short circuit, enabling broadcasts to start again.

Throughout this time normal Radio Caroline South programmes were still being broadcast from the *Cheeta 2* and some DJs from

Caroline North were brought south to help with the test transmissions from the *Mi Amigo*. For a few days there were two separate programmes being broadcast under the call sign of Caroline South, but at 6.00am on 27th April the *Mi Amigo* was able to resume responsibility for the station's regular programming. *Cheeta 2* then continued to relay these transmissions and DJ Robbie Dale stayed on board for a few days to make announcements asking listeners to re-tune to the new wavelength.

With a new powerful transmitter and new wavelength giving improved reception across southern Britain broadcasting hours were gradually increased and eventually Radio Caroline South became a 24 hour station for the first time.

In the 87 days which had elapsed between the *Mi Amigo* running aground on Frinton Beach and returning to her anchorage Radio Caroline South, despite having been loaned another fully equipped radio ship, had been off the air for a total of 43 days - and even when the station had been broadcasting it was on reduced power or reduced transmission hours (or both). Consequently Caroline South had suffered a further serious reduction in audience levels and lost yet more advertising revenue - only the income from Caroline North was keeping the network on the air and financially stable.

By contrast, Radio London had provided listeners and advertisers with a continuity of service and had built an even larger audience for itself in the absence of any real competition from its main rival. In April 1966 it was announced that Radio London's advertising revenue had exceeded £600,000 - 90% of which came from national advertisers.

The spring and summer of 1966 was a particularly active period for British offshore radio. As well as Radio Caroline South being re-launched on a new frequency and Radio Scotland moving from the east to west coast three new stations were due on air in April 1966.

The first, known as Radio 270, was to be based on a ship anchored off the Yorkshire coast serving the North East of England, Yorkshire and the East Midlands. The idea for this 'local' offshore station had originated in November 1965 when, inspired by the success of stations in the south, a group of businessmen got together to make plans for a similar operation to serve Yorkshire and the north east.

News of the project quickly spread and many local businessmen expressed an interest in using the services of the proposed station to advertise their company's products. Foremost amongst these was local supermarket owner, former RAF pilot and local MP, Wilf Proudfoot, who had approached all local advertising agencies to find out how he could buy airtime on the planned station to promote his stores. The station's backers invited Wilf Proudfoot to become involved financially in funding the station, an offer he readily accepted and went on to produce a financial business plan as well as persuading many other investors to put their money into the project.

Over the next few months the usual complicated web of offshore radio asset ownership and company registration arrangements were put in place to protect investors once the station had come on air. The radio station itself was registered in Panama as Progressiva Compania Commercial

SA, with Jack Lamont, the American film producer named as the company's principal director. An Australian, Noel Miller was appointed as the Panamanian company's British agent and he also later acted as senior DJ and Programme Director for the radio station. The holding company for the whole project, Ellambar Investments Ltd. was actually registered in Britain, but had 'loaned' its entire capital of £50,000 to Progressiva Compania Commercial S A.

The consortium purchased a former Dutch fishing vessel, the *Oceaan VII* and conversion work was carried out in the Channel Islands where two studios, and a 154' tall aerial mast were installed, together with generators and a 10Kw transmitter.

A very short timescale had been allowed for fitting out and equipping the station, with an on-air date of 1st April 1966 being planned - and almost achieved. A press conference was arranged in the Grand Hotel, Scarborough on that date with the intention that at 12 noon the station would come on air, witnessed by the assembled journalists, generating enormous publicity in the local and national press. However, the station did not achieve this

Oceaan VII at anchor off the Yorkshire coast

The Beat Fleet

RADIO 270

target and because of the date, the sceptical journalists treated the whole episode as an elaborate April Fools hoax.

Unfortunately for the project's embarrassed backers what happened out at sea was beyond their control. The *Oceaan VII* had sailed from Grimsby, where she had called for final fitting-out, but had encountered unseasonable bad weather and suffered some storm damage. The DJs and radio crew had set out from Scarborough in another vessel the previous night for a planned rendezvous at sea with *Oceaan VII*, taking with them a supply of records and other programme material. However, shortly after they had transferred to the *Oceaan VII* in the early hours of the morning a Force 7 gale blew up off the Yorkshire coast, and a 100' section of the aerial mast collapsed across the deck of the would-be radio ship.

Rough weather in the North Sea persisted for a few days, delaying the radio ship being towed back to Grimsby for repairs; which themselves took a lot longer than originally anticipated. It was not until early June that test transmissions for Radio 270 eventually started with full programmes beginning on 9th June. The station adopted a Top 40 format and tried to base its presentation style on the successful contemporary American Top 40 stations such as WABC, WMCA and WINS in New York. Unfortunately the slick presentation style of

the role models did not come easily to a team of largely English and Australian DJs who tried to effect a 'mid Atlantic' accent in their programme presentation and, from a listener's point of view, the overall effect was far from successful.

The station suffered technically, too, with a faulty power supply causing records and tapes to play at erratic speeds and there was a general lack of quality in the recording of commercials and jingles (many of the latter having been pirated off air from other offshore stations). During its first few weeks of broadcasting Radio 270 was frequently closed for 'essential maintenance', a euphemism for repeated generator failures, a problem which was to plague the station throughout its life even until its final few moments on the air 14 months later.

Before Radio 270 had opened the station announced that its programming would be aimed at a local audience and it did carry a significant amount of local advertising as well as community announcements and charity appeals. To encourage local businessmen to advertise the station introduced free introductory spots and suitably discounted rates for very small advertisers. Radio 270 also gave a lot of air time to charitable organisations such as local Rotary clubs, children's homes, the Royal National Lifeboat Institute, Oxfam, the Salvation Army, and Wireless for the Blind

A programme unique amongst the offshore radio stations was the "270 Swap Shop" where listeners wrote in with details of items they wanted to swap, together with their address or telephone number and this information was then broadcast free of charge.

Radio 270 programme schedule 1966

Radio 270 operated alternative schedules to account for DJ's shore leave:-

	Schedule A	Schedule B
6.30am	Leon Tippler Breakfast Show	Paul Burnett Breakfast Show
9.00am	Dennis the Menace Show	Roger Keene Show
12noon	The Neddy Noel Show	Boots Bowman Show
2.00pm	Dennis the Menace Show	Roger Keene Show
4.00pm	Neddy Noel Show	Boots Bowman Show
7.00pm	Hal Yorke Show	Paul Burnett Show
9.00pm	Andy Kirk Show	Alex Dee Show
12midnight	The Midnight Hour	The Midnight Hour
1.00am	Closedown	Closedown

One operational aspect, which was also unique to Radio 270, was the absence of a regular tendering vessel to deliver bulk supplies of food, fuel and water. When these were needed the *Oceaan VII* sailed into port, usually Bridlington Harbour, loaded whatever was required and returned to her anchorage in international waters. It was not unknown for transmissions to continue throughout these unannounced visits to port!

Remarkably, given the constant technical problems which blighted the station, its signal was reasonably strong in large areas of the north and Midlands. There were even reports from Lincolnshire that listeners in that area could not pick up their preferred station, Radio London, on the adjacent 266m wavelength because of the strength of Radio 270's signal!

A lavish press conference in London on 20th April 1966 announced the launch of yet another offshore radio project - the most ambitious so far, with two separate stations based on the same ship.

The new project was planning to start broadcasts from off the Essex coast by the end of April, but in fact test transmissions for the two new stations - Radio England and Britain Radio - did not take place until early May.

Although based on the same ship the twin stations were to be radically different from eachother and from any other offshore or landbased stations then on the air. Radio England, which planned to compete in the market area already covered by Radios Caroline, London and City, was to be a brash, all-American Top 40 format station, while Britain Radio, although still largely American in format, was to present easy listening music aimed at the same audience sector as Radio 390.

Behind this ambitious project were some of the original backers of Radio London who had broken away from Big L early in 1965 after fundamental boardroom differences over programming style and format. They had originally wanted to use Radio London to re-broadcast programmes from KLIF in Dallas. There was a strong body of feeling amongst them that Radio London should have projected a more undiluted American format rather than the watered down version which had been adopted for British audiences. Hence the launch of the new twin station project, whose ship, *Olga Patricia,* renamed *Laissez Faire,* had been a military landing craft and was fitted out for her new role in Miami.

Laissez Faire, home to twin stations Radio England and Britain Radio

After numerous delays and problems with the installation of equipment on the *Laissez Faire* test broadcasts started from the ship on 3rd May and to begin with Radio England used a wavelength of 355m, while Britain Radio used 227m, although the potential transmitter power of 55Kw for each station was not achieved due to continuing technical problems. For most of May 1966 test broadcasts were made sporadically on these

355 BRITAIN RADIO ENGLAND 227

wavelengths with regular interruptions and breakdowns while equipment was adjusted and modified. Regular programmes from both stations eventually started on 16th June.

Almost as soon as test transmissions had begun the Italian Government complained that Radio England was interfering with its Roma 2 station. As a result Britain Radio and Radio England swapped wavelengths while transmitter power was reduced significantly during the evenings. The Italian Government also complained to Panama about interference from the stations on board *Laissez Faire* and the ship's registration was withdrawn. The vessel remained a stateless ship for two months until she was re-registered in Honduras, but this information was not publicised at the time for fear of possible boarding by the authorities as well as violation of the ship's insurance cover.

Programming on Radio England (or Swinging Radio England as it was more usually known) was something entirely new to British audiences. It was undiluted and unashamedly American in style with fast talking DJs, known as "Boss Jocks", making much use of technical gimmicks such as echo and reverberation units, as well as an automated Musical Carousel unit - the first to be used in Europe.

This unit, similar in principle to a juke box, but working with tape cartridges instead of discs, could be used to provide either non-stop music automatically (as Radio England did at weekends with its "Golden Oldies" programme or Britain Radio did on its overnight service) or be incorporated into DJ controlled programmes. The equipment also stored commercials and station identification jingles on cartridges and had the ability, in response to a cue tone, to activate programmes recorded on reel to reel tapes. When each piece of music on the reel to reel tape ended another cue tone activated the carousel unit to insert further commercials or jingles automatically.

A number of DJs were hired from American Top 40 stations for Britain Radio and Radio England and to supplement this nucleus of American broadcasting staff some English DJs, who had little or no previous radio experience, were also recruited. The theory behind this policy was that the US DJs would be able to influence their inexperienced British colleagues in the style of presentation required on the stations, but at the same time the presence of some English voices would appeal to listeners more so than a totally American team. This policy was later to lead to a serious conflict between the two groups, helping to undermine the success of the whole project and in particular Radio England.

Much US chart material, including some from artists unknown in Britain, was played on Radio England and a daily taped programme, hosted by DJ Gary Stevens, from New York station WMCA contained American music and links which was either not understood or largely not of any interest or relevance to British audiences.

Radio England also brought with it jingles which had been custom-made for the station by Promotion and Marketing Services (PAMS) of Dallas, Texas. These jingles were intended to give the station a clear identity and help to establish it in the increasingly competitive British offshore radio market. Somewhat naively, however, Radio England played these jingles during test transmissions without voice over interruption from DJs. Most of the other contemporary offshore stations then recorded the jingles, edited them to include their own identification and used them during their own programmes before the new station was able to begin regular broadcasts. The effect of this was that when it did begin officially, Radio England sounded as though it was using the same jingles as all the other stations and had nothing original of its own, when in fact the reverse was true.

Radio England programme schedule June 1966

6.00am	Ron O'Quinn Show
10.00am	Larry Dean Show
2.00pm	Gerry Smithwick Show
6.00pm	Roger Day Show
10.00pm	Rick Randall Show
2.00am	Graham Gill Show

News and weather at 15 minutes past the hour
Weather at 15 minutes to the hour

To combat this Radio England quickly acquired another jingle package using the "Batman" theme, which at that time was a popular cult television series.

Although the station's audience in July 1966, one month after coming on air, was recorded in an NOP survey as 2,274,000 Radio England's format never really caught on with audiences, advertisers or even its own English DJs. There was constant friction between the English and American staff on board the *Laissez Faire* - the Americans thought the English naive and inexperienced in broadcasting matters, while the English accused the Americans of misreading British audience tastes and trying to impose undiluted US format radio. This conflict eventually resulted in the 'resignation' of four of the original American "Boss Jocks" in September after they became totally disillusioned with the operation of the station.

To compound the station's problems, initial commercial contracts were, by and large, not renewed by dissatisfied advertisers and as a consequence the American backers decided the station was not generating a sufficient return on their investment. Coupled with this slump in advertising revenue the station mounted a huge nationwide tour - "Swinging 66", with artists such as The Small Faces, Crispian St. Peters, Neil Christian, Dave Berry and (in the London venues) Wayne Fontana. The tour was hosted by Radio England DJs Larry Dean, Jerry Smethwick and Roger Day, but after two disastrous London concerts Roger Day was left to compere the rest of the venues alone.

"Swinging 66" was booked to appear at venues which included towns and cities well outside Radio England's transmission area and highlighted, yet again, how the station's American backers had misjudged the British market. They claimed, and probably genuinely believed, that the twin stations operating from the *Laissez Faire* gave national coverage, but in reality Radio England and Britain Radio's daytime signals hardly reached beyond the Midlands. As a consequence people turning up, by chance, at venues in the north of England or even Scotland, knew little or nothing about Radio England and any on-air promotions were completely wasted because the station's signal did not reach those areas.

Overall the tour was a massive and costly failure, bringing even further financial problems for the station. Another problem left over from the Tour was how to dispose of some 50,000 unsold concert programmes, so it was decided to offer them for sale 'autographed' by pop stars who had participated in "Swinging 66". They were extensively advertised on Radio England, but it subsequently came to light that most of the 'autographs' were copies signed by the station's secretarial and office staff. Only about 1,000 of the programmes were sold in this promotion - another costly loss to the station.

In contrast to Radio England its sister station, Britain Radio catered for a quieter, mature audience. This station also brought with it a set of custom-made jingles to help create its identity in the market place - "Hallmark of Quality - Britain Radio". Fortunately for Britain Radio these were not pirated by rival stations, as happened with the Radio England package.

Although it was supposedly catering for the same audience sector as Radio 390, Britain Radio adopted an entirely different programming style. Instead of the 15 and 30 minute segments of specialist music, which Radio 390 had so successfully tailored for its audience, Britain Radio adopted the same 'horizontal' format as its pop rivals using three or four hour programmes, but with the DJ's playing easy listening music instead of Top 40 pop.

Britain Radio programme schedule

6.00am	Breakfast Club
7.00am	The World Tomorrow
7.30am	Breakfast Club
9.00am	Morning Serenade
12noon	Musical Carousel
12.30pm	The World Tomorrow
1.00pm	Musical Carousel
4.00pm	Rush Hours
6.00pm	Evening Spin
7.00pm	R & B Nite Ride *(Sundays)*
8.00pm	Late Date
12midnight`	Closedown

News and weather every hour, on the hour

Unfortunately audiences and advertisers were not won over - the July 1966 NOP survey showed Britain Radio's listenership as only 718,000 compared with Radio 390's 2,633,000.

Despite its apparent failure to appeal to British audiences and advertisers Britain Radio can lay claim to having achieved two offshore radio 'firsts'. One of its initial advertisers, Sunbake Bakeware, used the station to launch a new range of products in a series of commercials broadcast in English, French, Dutch and German. It was not the use of a multi-language approach which made these commercials unique (both Radio London and Radio Caroline had aired French and Dutch language commercials before), but rather it was the fact that for the first time an advertiser had chosen to use offshore radio (and a new station at that) to mount a campaign for the launch of a new product, a practice normally reserved for established and proven media outlets.

The other landmark for Britain Radio was the first political advertisement broadcast on a British offshore radio station. This happened on 29th September 1966, when Mr. M McLaren - the Ratepayer's candidate in a by-election for Harwich Town Council - bought airtime on Britain Radio. He was able to do this because the Representation of the People Act 1947, which requires that broadcasters give equal airtime to all candidates standing in an election, did not apply as the station operated outside British jurisdiction. As a matter of record Mr. McLaren won the by-election, but it is impossible to accurately attribute his success solely to the advertisements on Britain Radio.

As well as all this activity in 1966 from newcomers to the offshore radio business some of the established stations were also planning expansion in the continued absence of definite action from the Government to suppress them.

Radio 390 had plans to expand during the spring and summer of 1966 when the station's Managing Director, Ted Allbeury, opened negotiations with Britt Wadner, owner of the former Scandinavian station Radio Syd, to purchase her radio ship, *Cheeta 2,* which was then lying at anchor off Harwich having fulfilled her role earlier that year as a temporary home for Radio Caroline South. Although others, notably Radio London, had looked at the possibility of purchasing *Cheeta 2* nothing had ever been concluded and because of tougher laws passed in Sweden at the beginning of 1966 there was now no possibility that Radio Syd could ever return to the air from its former Scandinavian anchorage.

The plan was to anchor the *Cheeta 2* off the coast of the Wirral peninsular in the north west of England to broadcast 'sweet music' programmes under the call sign Radio 390 North. With the original station on Red Sands Fort renamed Radio 390 South, this would have given listeners and advertisers an easy listening station with almost national coverage and an alternative to Radio Caroline's national pop music service.

Radio 390's expansion plans reached such an advanced stage that rate cards were printed and circulated to agencies and potential advertisers detailing plans for the introduction of Radio 390 North and a VHF (FM) service in the south. However, differences of opinion amongst the Radio 390 board of directors and later prosecutions brought against the station by the authorities combined to prevent these plans being put into practice.

Cheeta 2 also suddenly became unavailable at about this time. The vessel had been moored off Harwich since ending her service with Radio Caroline South, but in mid-July she dragged her anchor in heavy seas and had to be towed into port. Here a writ of attachment was nailed to her mast by creditors and she was impounded by the Admiralty Marshall pending the outcome of an outstanding salvage claim.

Radio London also planned to follow Radio Caroline's example and establish a sister station serving the north of England from an anchorage in the Irish Sea, using the call sign Radio Manchester. Staff from Radio London even examined the *Cheeta 2* after Radio Caroline South had finished using her, with a view to the ship becoming the base for Radio Manchester, but the vessel was found to be in such an unseaworthy condition that this idea was not pursued.

In April 1966 Radio London opened negotiations with Radio City proposing a take over of the fort-based station to re-launch it as an easy listening service to rival Radio 390 and the recently announced Britain Radio, using the call sign UKGM - United Kingdom Good Music.

A deal was struck in May under which Radio London would manage the UKGM operation and take 55% of its advertising revenue, while Radio City would retain ownership of the station and all its equipment on Shivering Sands Fort. In addition both stations (Radio London and UKGM) would have a joint servicing and tendering arrangement as well as a combined advertising sales company. It was planned that the agreement would come into effect on 1st June and that UKGM would become fully operational from 1st July.

Early in June two DJs from Radio London, Keith Skues and Duncan Johnson together with Office Manager Dennis Maitland, went to Shivering Sands Fort to assess the condition of Radio City's transmitter and studio equipment. At about the same time all City's DJs were invited to Radio London's headquarters in Curzon Street to be told of the plans for UKGM and offered jobs on the new station.

However, the merger plans did not go ahead as envisaged. It came to light that, as well as negotiating this deal with Radio London, Radio City's owner, Reg Calvert, had secretly continued to have parallel negotiations with Major Oliver Smedley of Project Atlanta - the original organisation behind Radio Atlanta in 1964 which also had links with Radio Caroline

from July 1964 until December 1965. Previous negotiations between these two men had resulted in the joint Radio Caroline/Radio City advertising sales fiasco in September 1965 and the delivery of an obsolete transmitter to the Shivering Sands Fort by a team from Project Atlanta.

In these latest negotiations Smedley offered Calvert £10,000 cash for Project Atlanta to purchase Radio City outright or, alternatively, the equivalent amount of shares in a joint operating company. Reg Calvert remained non-committal to this offer while at the same time continuing his clandestine negotiations with Radio London, which eventually culminated in the UKGM proposal.

Plans for the launch of UKGM were first made public in a newspaper article on 16th June 1966. Oliver Smedley, reading for the first time of this agreement between Radio London and Radio City, feared that he was being double crossed by Reg Calvert and that his Project Atlanta transmitter on Shivering Sands (for which he had still not been paid by Calvert) would be put to use by the new easy-listening station.

Smedley hurriedly arranged a boarding party to go out to Shivering Sands Fort to reclaim his transmitting equipment. On Shivering Sands Fort Radio City had closed for the day and the seven broadcasting and engineering staff were all asleep as Smedley and the boarding party of seventeen hired men scrambled onto the structure in the early hours of 20th June, successfully occupying it and meeting no resistance whatsoever. The transmitter crystal was removed and taken ashore by Smedley, while the remainder of the boarding party were left in occupation of Shivering Sands with the Radio City staff locked in their quarters unable to put their station on air as usual.

In the meantime Oliver Smedley drove to the home of Radio London's Managing Director, Philip Birch, and confronted him outside his house when a heated conversation took place. The two men eventually agreed that they should meet again later that same day at Project Atlanta's offices in Dean Street, London.

On the day after his station had been silenced, Reg Calvert reported the raid to police at

Scotland Yard. The police were uncertain whether or not they could take any action because they thought that Shivering Sands Fort was outside British territorial limits.

Having received no assistance from the police Reg Calvert drove, later that same evening, to Major Oliver Smedley's house near Saffron Walden, Essex and entered the house by forcing his way past Smedley's housekeeper and secretary, Pamela Thorburn. A scuffle developed between the two men in the hall and the sitting room and Calvert then picked up a marble bust with which he threatened Miss Thorburn, eventually throwing it to the ground and smashing it into fragments.

While the struggle between Reg Calvert and Miss Thorburn had been going on Oliver Smedley had gone to ask his neighbour to telephone the police. Smedley returned to his house, picked up a shotgun and in the struggle with Calvert fired a shot which killed him.

Major Oliver Smedley was arrested at his cottage and the following morning formally charged with murdering Calvert. When he appeared before a special court in Saffron Walden Smedley's solicitor told Magistrates that his client completely denied the charge of murder and, after a five minute hearing, he was remanded in custody for a further eight days.

The same day as Smedley's Court appearance police went out to Shivering Sands to question the seven Radio City staff and members of the boarding party who were still occupying the Fort. They left after three and a half hours having taken statements, but without making any arrests.

On 23rd June Reg Calvert's widow, Dorothy, appeared on television stating that she hoped to have Radio City back on the air in two or three days time. She also announced that the negotiations to sell Radio City, which had been taking place before her husband's death, were now in abeyance.

Then without warning on Sunday 26th June, exactly a week after arriving, the boarding party left Shivering Sands Fort. Using a spare transmitter crystal which had been hidden from the boarders, Radio City started test transmissions again at 9.30pm that evening and by 10.00pm the station was back on the air.

Major Oliver Smedley appeared in Court again on 18th July and after a 50 minute retirement the Magistrates decided to grant bail and commit him for trial at Chelmsford Assizes, but on a reduced charge of manslaughter rather than murder. At the two day hearing in Chelmsford on 11th October the sequence of events and the circumstances surrounding the boarding of Shivering Sands Fort were related to the Court. Oliver Smedley's solicitor again argued that his client had acted in self defence, protecting himself, his housekeeper and his home from a violent intruder. The jury, without retiring to consider the evidence presented to them, returned a 'not guilty ' verdict and Oliver Smedley left court a free man.

These dramatic events did much to shatter the fun packed, 'pirate' image of the offshore radio stations, revealing a ruthless world of double-dealing, financial intrigue, physical violence and death threats.

In Parliament MPs pressed the Government to take action against offshore broadcasters in the light of the boarding of Shivering Sands Fort and the subsequent shooting of Reg Calvert. Postmaster General Anthony Wedgewood Benn initially told the House of Commons that the Government's Bill to outlaw offshore stations was ready to be introduced, but this would not happen immediately because of possible prosecutions arising from the Radio City affair and the death of the station's owner.

However, on 1st July 1966 it was announced that legislation to outlaw offshore radio stations would now be introduced before the summer recess - in the light of events at Radio City the Government had rearranged its parliamentary timetable. The Postmaster General also indicated that the Government was contemplating a "general review of broadcasting policy" which would include "the better provision of popular music on a national basis as well as the establishment of local public service radio stations."

The events on Radio City and the subsequent questions in the House of Commons at the end of June 1966 had brought into sharp focus the Government's failure on two fronts to act against the offshore stations. Firstly to take some positive action against the fort-based broadcasters who, despite all their assertions to the contrary, **were** illegally occupying Government-owned properties, which by virtue of the provisions of a 1964 Order in Council, were inside territorial waters

Secondly the Labour Government had continued with its Conservative predecessor's procrastinations, claiming higher legislative priorities and lack of parliamentary time - despite Britain having ratified the Strasbourg Convention provisions to outlaw offshore broadcasting in January 1965. As a further reason for not introducing anti-offshore radio legislation the Government relied on its vague promise to undertake a "general review" of broadcasting policy, including the creation of a legal alternative to the 'pirate' stations as well as a public service based local radio network.

In this atmosphere of apparent immunity from official action the offshore stations had flourished and multiplied throughout late 1965 and early 1966. However, the Radio City affair, with its graphic demonstration of anarchic and violent behaviour spelt the beginning of the end for all British offshore broadcasters - the Government could no longer be seen to delay taking action to deal with a situation which was rapidly deteriorating and becoming out of control.

Two days after the announcement that legislation would now be introduced before the summer recess Postmaster General Anthony Wedgewood Benn was replaced in a Cabinet reshuffle by a new Minister, Edward Short. He was to adopt a far more positive and aggressive attitude towards outlawing the offshore broadcasters and a few days after taking up his appointment Mr. Short announced that broadcasting in Britain was to remain firmly under public control and, once they had been closed, the offshore stations would not be replaced by local commercial stations.

Frinton Flashing

Anchored just three and a half miles off Frinton-on-Sea, Essex, DJs on the Caroline South ship could see land on a clear day, but at night any lights along the sea front were very clearly visible, weather permitting.

Johnnie Walker, who presented the 9-12 midnight programme is probably best remembered for Frinton Flashing. Motorists would park their cars along the seafront with their headlights directed at the radio ship. At the request of the DJ they would be asked to flash their headlights in response to questions - names, registration numbers, dates of birth etc.

Other DJs on deck would relay information about the responses to the on-air DJ and by a process of elimination this would be whittled down to one, two or three vehicles.

After Frinton Flashing sessions were over Johnnie Walker introduced the 'kiss in the car' session, playing a long, slow, romantic piece of music to create the right atmosphere!

JAN 68
RADIO CAROLINE
Johnnie Walker
OFFICIAL
KISS·IN·THE·CAR
LICENCE

Vox Pop

I can still remember Johnnie Walker and Frinton Flashing.

My boyfriend at the time had a Ford Consul and we used to drive to the promenade at Frinton and flash the headlights at Radio Caroline, following Johnnie's instructions

There were others all along the promenade doing the same - it must have been quite a sight from the ship for Johnnie to see all those headlights 'talking' to him.

I remember one occasion when he tried to find out somebody's name by asking them to spell out the letters with flashes - once for A, twice for B etc. I think he established the girl's name, but it wasn't me!

Lynne (Colchester, Essex)

The Bill to outlaw offshore broadcasting stations - the Marine etc. Broadcasting (Offences) Bill (M.O.B.) was eventually introduced into the House of Commons on 27th July 1966 and received its formal First Reading. The provisions contained in the Bill applied to all structures, floating, fixed or airborne, which could be used as bases for broadcasting and prohibited any British citizen or company from owning, operating, working for, supplying, advertising on or in any way assisting an offshore station. Penalties for contravening the Bill's provisions were £100 fines or three months imprisonment, or both on conviction in a Magistrates Court, or two years in prison and an unspecified fine on conviction at Quarter Sessions or Assizes (now Crown Courts).

The offshore stations' initial reactions to the Bill were defiant, containing general expressions of determination to fight its introduction and continue broadcasting.

Radio Caroline condemned the Bill as "spiteful, unimaginative and a negation of basic freedom that seeks to put an outright ban on the enjoyment of 25 million regular listeners to offshore radio, without submitting any alternative proposals for satisfying the legitimate demand." At the same time the station engaged a public relations company to help it fight the legislation when Parliament reassembled in the autumn.

Radio City owner Dorothy Calvert said she hoped enough MPs in Parliament would realise that the offshore stations were giving the public a service they wanted and would throw the Bill out.

Bill Vick of **Radio England/Britain Radio** said "our ship is American owned and crewed, and the DJs are American. I have already been approached by several continental businessmen about advertising."

Radio Essex owner Roy Bates said he would live abroad to escape the provisions of the planned legislation.

Radio London's Managing Director, Philip Birch promised to move the station's headquarters abroad, to supply the ship from Spain and Holland and obtain advertising from New York and Paris. He went on to state that the Bill would discriminate against British manufacturers who would no longer be able to use Radio London to advertise their products. Radio London, he said, would still be broadcasting in 30 years time.

Radio Scotland claimed to have a plan to continue broadcasting by supplying the *Comet* from Ireland, moving its anchorage 70 miles out into the Atlantic, installing a more powerful transmitter and replacing the Scottish crew and DJs with foreign staff. The station organised a petition and within a month two and a half million signatures had been collected.

Radio 270 Managing Director, Wilf Proudfoot promised that his station would find ways of getting round the legislation, if it ever succeeded in progressing beyond the First Reading stage. The station launched a campaign urging listeners to write to their MPs and 'fight for free radio'.

A **Radio 390** spokesman said that the station would use the former Radio Syd ship, *Cheeta 2* as a base from which to continue its broadcasts if the Government took action against them on the Red Sands Fort. The station would, he said, meet the salvage claim outstanding on the vessel and release her from Harwich. The 'sweet music' station also exhorted its listeners to write to their MPs protesting against the proposed legislation.

In the House of Commons opposition to the M.O.B. was immediate. The day after the Bill's First Reading a motion was tabled by two Conservative MPs which stated that "the Bill will deprive millions of people of the sound of music they love and can at present only get from the pirate stations". Another Conservative MP, Eldon Griffiths, called on the Postmaster General to "make speedy provision for legitimate local broadcasting stations to meet the British people's evident desire for a wider range and greater variety of broadcasting than is at present available from the BBC."

Some stations, however, did not have to wait for the introduction of the legislation proposed in the M.O.B. before action was taken against them. On 21st September 1966 summonses were served by the Post Office on Estuary Radio Ltd., the owners of Radio 390, alleging that "on 16th August at Red Sands Tower, situated eight and a half miles off the coast but within the Thames Estuary, the company did unlawfully use apparatus for wireless telegraphy, namely a transmitter, contrary to section 1 of the Wireless Telegraphy Act 1949".

A week later Roy Bates of Radio Essex, was served with a similar summons alleging the illegal use of a transmitter at Knock John Fort, again contravening the Wireless Telegraphy Act. Roy Bates then announced that he had taken over another fort at Tongue Sands, nine miles off Margate, and would use this as a broadcasting base for a new station - to be known either as Radio Albatross or Radio Kent. Then at the beginning of October the name and format of Radio Essex was changed to BBMS (Britain's Better Music Station), which now broadcast easy listening music during the day and pop at night.

The other fort-based station, Radio City, remained un-summonsed at this stage, but surprisingly a ship-based station, Radio Scotland, was served with a summons in December 1966 alleging that it had broadcast within territorial waters from its anchorage off Troon on the west coast of Scotland. The basis for this prosecution, which eventually came to court in March 1967, lay in a complicated legal argument about the definition of a bay, but in effect the *Comet* was allegedly anchored inside British territorial waters.

When the Radio 390 case came to be heard at Canterbury on 24th November the Post Office gave evidence from three of its engineers that the station's transmissions had been monitored and recorded at three separate locations. The case centred not just on the fact that the broadcasts had taken place, but whether in fact Red Sands Fort was within British territorial waters. Sir Peter Rawlinson QC, appearing on behalf of Estuary Radio Ltd. stated that the Fort was at least six miles off the Kent coast and therefore outside territorial waters.

The Post Office argued that under the terms of an Order in Council the Thames Estuary can

be considered a 'bay'. To substantiate this the Post Office further argued that low tide elevations - which determine the starting point for calculating British territorial waters - include all 'islands' uncovered at low water. It was claimed that because Middle Bank, a sandbank off the Isle of Sheppey, was regularly uncovered at low tide it met this provision and, therefore, formed the baseline from which the extent of territorial waters could be calculated.

The magistrates found that the Post Office had proved its case and fined Estuary Radio Ltd. £100 for using an unlicensed transmitter inside territorial waters, but an application for the confiscation of transmitting equipment and the award of costs was refused.

Although immediately giving notice of appeal against the Court's decision Radio 390's Managing Director, Ted Allbeury announced that, pending the outcome of that hearing, the station would have to close. So at 11.00pm on 25th November Radio 390 played a tape recorded message from Mr. Allbeury in which he explained to listeners the reasons for the station having to go off the air. The duty announcer then said "This is Radio 390 now closing down." and the station closed in the usual manner by playing the National Anthem.

Five days later, Roy Bates of Radio Essex appeared at Rochford Magistrates Court to answer similar charges that he had used an unlicensed transmitter for radio broadcasting at the Knock John Fort. The same arguments

THANKS FOR YOUR REPORT.
RADIO ESSEX
ON 222 METRES
ARE ALWAYS PLEASED TO HEAR FROM YOU!

which had been successfully presented the previous week by the Post Office against Radio 390 were re-stated - that the Thames Estuary was a bay and the West Barrow sandbank gave a low tide elevation which brought the Knock John Fort inside territorial waters. The Post Office engineers also gave evidence of monitoring Radio Essex transmissions from three separate locations.

Roy Bates, appearing on his own behalf, argued that his station was outside the jurisdiction of the Court because it was located

majority of 2 to 1) that the provisions of the Order in Council of 1964 **did** have the effect of bringing Red Sands Fort inside British territorial waters and, as a consequence, the station had been illegally transmitting from that location. Lord Justice Salmon disagreed with the view of his two colleagues and it was suggested that Estuary Radio Ltd. could take the case to the House of Lords for final determination. However, Ted Allbeury decided that it would be too costly, and ultimately pointless, to take the appeal to the House of Lords and, therefore, Radio 390 would stay off the air.

BBMS programme schedule

	Weekdays	Weekends
6.00am	Daybreak Programme	Weekend Special
9.00am	Morning Melody	Morning Melody
12noon	Musical Magazine	Musical Magazine
2.00pm		Swing Session
3.00pm	Music 'till Six	Afternoon Spin
5.00pm		Country and Western *(Sat)*
		Jazz Along An Hour *(Sun)*
6.00pm	Swing Session	Swing Session
7.00pm	Evening Inn	Evening Inn
9.00pm	Formula 67	Formula 67

Meanwhile, Radio Caroline, having distanced itself from the Radio City affair by issuing a press release stating that all connections with Project Atlanta and Major Oliver Smedley had been severed in 1965, continued to consolidate and improve its own programme format.

more than three nautical miles off the Essex coast. However, the magistrates found that the Knock John Fort was within British territorial waters and imposed a fine of £100, but refused a Post Office request for confiscation of transmitting equipment and payment of costs.

Mr. Bates immediately lodged an appeal but his station, BBMS did not cease transmissions, as Radio 390 had done after its conviction instead, against the advice of his solicitor, he decided to keep his station on the air from the Knock John Fort. However, with no money and an absence of almost any advertising income since September, BBMS was only able to struggle on for a few more weeks, eventually closing at Christmas 1966.

Radio 390's appeal against conviction was heard in the High Court on 12th December 1966 before the Lord Chief Justice, Lord Parker, sitting with Lord Justice Salmon and Mr. Justice Blain. Estuary Radio Ltd., seeking to have its conviction by Canterbury Magistrates quashed,was again represented by Sir Peter Rawlinson QC.

After hearing the arguments presented by both sides the Court ruled the following day (by a

Following the refurbishment of the *Mi Amigo,* the introduction of a new wavelength (259m) and a more powerful transmitter in May 1966 the output from Caroline South improved enormously under the guidance of new Programme Director, Tom Lodge, who had been brought down from the North ship by Ronan O'Rahilly.

Tom Lodge recruited a new team of DJs, many without previous radio experience, but who displayed enthusiasm in their presentation style and an empathy for the music they were playing. Under Tom Lodge's direction Caroline North had programmed successfully since arriving off the Isle of Man in July 1964 and he introduced the same style to the South ship during 1966. As a result Caroline South started to sound a far more interesting radio station and more in touch with its audience's musical demands than had previously been the case.

Despite all these programming adjustments one big weakness still remained - a lack of substantial advertising income. Many big advertisers were still preferring to spend their money with Radio London while Radio Caroline (and Caroline South in particular), although attracting some major brand names, had to rely heavily on small advertisers or in-house promotions for T-shirts, fashion jewellery or Caroline Club membership to fill its commercial airtime.

In August 1966 Ronan O'Rahilly engaged two consultants to revamp the Caroline Sales organisation and generate more advertising income for the station. Terry Bate (who had worked very successfully in Canadian commercial radio) and Alan Slaight were charged with the task of selling airtime, creating commercial opportunities, promoting in-house merchandise and generally advising on sales administration.

One of the consultant's first objectives was to cut overheads and costs by drastically reducing the size of the Sales Department at Caroline House, while at the same time managing to achieve a larger volume of airtime sales. Terry Bate was also credited with the introduction of one of the most successful sponsorship deals ever achieved by an offshore radio station - "Caroline Cash Casino".

The concept of this promotion was that a large cash prize was offered to listeners who successfully solved clues broadcast during the 'Cash Casino' slots - aired hourly from 9.00am to 1.00pm each day. Major brand names sponsored the competition including Weetabix, Findus Frozen Foods, Galaxy Chocolate, VP Wines, Nabisco Shredded Wheat, Alberto VO5 Shampoo and Libby's

Canned Fruit products. Listeners were required to submit a product proof of purchase (usually a carton flap or bottle label) with their Cash Casino entries and Radio Caroline used these to demonstrate to individual sponsors the enormous success of the promotion.

The Cash Casino programme segments, hosted by DJ Bill Hearne, were taped at Caroline House and aired simultaneously on both the North and South ships. Each segment had a different sponsor and contained a new clue (in the form of a rhyming couplet) each day. Listener's answers were 'drawn' during each segment and £10 was added to the jackpot total for every incorrect answer.

Jackpot prizes awarded in the Caroline Cash Casino promotion ranged from £460 to £4,070 and during ten separate competitions a total of £26,190 was won by listeners. At the height of the competition the basement of Caroline House was filled with mail sacks bulging with listener's entries, a demonstration in itself of the enormous popularity of the Cash Casino feature. Within the first eleven weeks of the competition over one million entries were received with product proofs of purchase showing the following breakdown for each of the four original sponsors:-

Alberto VO5 Shampoo	99,840
Findus Frozen Foods	174,491
Libbys Canned Fruits	424,228
Weetabix Breakfast Cereal	394,216

Other major sponsorship deals were also arranged by Terry Bate including "Lucky Birthday Bonanza" (sponsored by Golden Wonder Peanuts), and "Partners in Profit" (sponsored by Weetabix and Ajax), all of which gave Caroline, and in particular Caroline South, a far more commercially successful sound, generated much needed income and heightened audience awareness of the station.

Radio Caroline North, meanwhile, had continued uninterrupted broadcasting throughout 1966 and, apart from the loan of some DJs to assist with test transmissions from the refurbished *Mi Amigo* in April, the station had remained relatively unscathed by all the troubles affecting her sister in the south. During the summer plans were announced to increase the transmitter power of Caroline North to

Vox Pop

Everybody talked about Cash Casino at school, trying to guess the answer from those rhyming clues.

At morning break one of the girls who had smuggled a transistor radio into school would listen to Radio Caroline to find out if anyone had won the jackpot while we had been in lessons.

Gwen (Prestatyn, North Wales)

50Kw and for a change in wavelength for the station to 259m, bringing it in line with Caroline South.

The practical difficulties of changing wavelength and increasing transmitter power while at the same time maintaining a normal daily programme schedule were tremendous. Radio Caroline North achieved both by closing its normal service on 199m at the usual time each evening and re-opening an hour later with test broadcasts throughout the night on 259m.

Offshore wedding

Yet another offshore radio 'first' was achieved by Radio Caroline North during September 1966 when one of the station's DJs, Mick Luvzit (Brown) was married on board the MV *Caroline* to Janet Teret, sister of another DJ, Ray Teret.

The ceremony which was conducted by the Captain of the MV *Caroline*, Martin Gips, under Panamanian law (as that was the country of registration of the radioship) was broadcast live during the afternoon of 21st September 1966.

These tests started at the end of October and continued into early December with a full daytime test on the new frequency on 23rd November. The permanent change to the new wavelength was completed on Sunday 18th December and Radio Caroline North then joined her sister station broadcasting under the national call sign "Caroline on 259".

After some weeks of speculation and rumours an announcement was made in mid-October 1966 that Radio England would be closing and the station's frequency leased to a Dutch language broadcaster, under the call sign Radio Dolifjn.

Radio England had not been the commercial success its American backers had hoped - the programming format was too brash for British audiences and, with a declining listenership, advertisers could not be persuaded to buy airtime on the station. In addition there had been constant professional friction between the American and British DJs on board the *Laissez Faire* and the disillusionment of those still on board was clearly evident in the station's final few hours until it closed at midnight on 5th November 1966. Although Britain Radio had been even less successful in audience terms than its sister station its own transmissions were not affected by the closure of Radio England and, for the time being the easy listening station continued to broadcast much as before.

The following day the Dutch language station, Radio Dolifjn took to the air broadcasting for eighteen hours a day. The station's format was similar to that of Britain Radio, with a number of Dutch DJs presenting programmes live from the *Laissez Faire*. Radio Dolifjn, nicknamed 'Flipper Radio' built up a small audience in Holland but never posed a real commercial threat to the longer established and far more popular pop music format of Radio Veronica which had been operating off the Dutch coast since 1960.

Towards the end of 1966 the BBC began to fuel the debate about how to eliminate the British offshore radio stations. In November it published the results of a survey, carried out by its own Audience Research Department and based on a sample of 5,000 people nationwide. This survey claimed to show that:-

(a) more than three quarters of the population over 15 never or hardly ever listened to the offshore stations;
(b) the BBC Light Programme had a daily audience four times greater than the total of the offshore stations' audience and
(c) the daily audience for offshore stations amounted to only 6,250,000.

The results of this survey can be contrasted with the one carried out by NOP the previous July which, although concentrating on commercial radio listenership as opposed to BBC, showed a substantially higher overall audience level for the offshore stations. The survey results showed the following figures for all adults:-

Station	Listenership
Radio Caroline	8,818,000
Radio Luxembourg	8,818,000
Radio London	8,140,000
Radio 390	2,633,000
Radio England	2,274,000
Radio Scotland	2,195,000
Britain Radio	718,000
TOTAL RADIO AUDIENCE	39,900,000

The BBC produced some further anti-offshore radio information in its Annual Report for 1965/66 which stated that the stations were spoiling reception of continental radio stations and "stealing the legal property of British musicians, gramophone companies and other copyright holders." The Report went on "Although willing to do so, the BBC has not been free to provide such a service on its legally allocated frequencies since it has to use its three networks to serve the community as a whole." This statement was a clear indication that the BBC were exploring means by which they could introduce an alternative to the offshore stations, but they were also experiencing resistance from organisations such as the Musicians Union and even some members of the Government who reportedly were in favour of establishing a separate radio organisation to provide a continuous pop music service.

However, the long awaited White Paper on the Future of Broadcasting, published in December 1966, proposed that the BBC should be authorised to operate a popular music service, using one of the existing wavelengths allocated to the Light Programme (247m) and also launch nine experimental local radio stations using VHF (FM) frequencies only.

This second proposal was a defeat for the local commercial radio lobby, which did not just consist of offshore radio station operators but a large number of community and business based groups who, for many years, had argued in favour of a commercially funded alternative to the BBC.

The White Paper firmly rejected any suggestion that local radio should be operated by commercial interests, stating -"It is of first importance to maintain public service principles in the further development of the broadcasting service."

At a press conference to launch the White Paper the Postmaster General, Edward Short, emphasised the point that the local radio experiment should not be commercially funded - "We have excluded this. We feel it is incompatible with the objective of a local radio station, which would be to contribute to the communal life of the town. I do not think you can reconcile this with commercial interests."

The offshore stations and other commercial radio interests reacted angrily to the White Paper proposals. Radio Caroline called it a "manifesto for monopolists" and a spokesman for the station went on to say, "It does little but perpetuate the dreariness of British broadcasting which the public has clearly rejected in its enthusiasm for the offshore stations." The Secretary of the Local Radio Association, John Gorst, said his organisation completely disagreed with the White Paper's proposals and that the limitation of the nine local stations to VHF (FM) would mean that just 11% of the population would be able to receive their transmissions.

1966 closed on a somewhat depressed note as far as offshore radio was concerned. Two stations had been closed as the result of prosecutions, another prosecution was pending and both the Government and the BBC had revealed their own plans which clearly offered no long-term future for the offshore broadcasters.

Dateline Diamonds

During the summer of 1965 the Radio London ship, *Galaxy*, became the set for a film - "Dateline Diamonds".

The film's storyline centred around a blackmailer who also became involved in diamond smuggling operations using a fictitious offshore radio station as a base.

The film starred William Lucas, Kenneth Cope, George Mikell, Conrad Phillips, Patsy Rowlands and Anna Carteret. Radio London DJ Kenny Everett also appeared in many scenes.

Dateline Diamonds was directed by Jeremy Sumners, produced by Harold Shampan and Harry Benn with screenplay by Tudor Gates. Music in the film was supplied by The Small Faces, The Chantelles and Kiki Dee.

Chapter 8   The fight for Free Radio

1967 started with the return of a station which had closed the previous November. Radio 390 started to broadcast again at midnight on 31st December 1966, claiming it had new evidence to show that its base at Red Sands Fort was at least one and a half miles outside British territorial waters.

During the prosecution of Estuary Radio Ltd. the Post Office had relied on the exposure, at low tide, of Middle Sands sandbank to determine a starting point for the calculation of the three mile territorial limit. Radio 390 had now taken measurements of its own and was satisfied that the Middle Sands sandbank was, in fact, never fully exposed at low tide.

However, optimism that this new evidence would successfully persuade the authorities that the station operated outside British jurisdiction was not shared by everyone. Managing Director Ted Allbeury resigned from the company on 10th February 1967 saying "I honestly believe a ship has greater potential than the Forts. The Forts are constantly being harassed by the Government. I have not been able to persuade my shareholders to take a ship and am therefore hamstrung to continue."

Two days later it was announced that he had joined Britain Radio, which he intended to re-launch with a format similar to Radio 390 and that he had taken with him a number of the fort-based station's announcers. Meanwhile David Lye, Company Secretary of Estuary Radio, took over as Acting Managing Director of Radio 390.

Following the recommencement of broadcasts the Post Office wasted no time in issuing new summonses against Radio 390, again alleging the illegal use of transmitting equipment within British territorial waters. On 23rd February magistrates at Southend heard a total of 28 summonses alleging that the station had broadcast without a licence from inside territorial limits on four occasions in January 1967.

During the hearing representatives of the Royal Navy were called by the prosecution to give evidence that the sandbank at Middle Sands was indeed exposed at low tide. They produced a photograph to the Court showing Lt. Commander John Mackay standing on the exposed sandbank holding a Union Jack flag which he had firmly planted in the sand. At the end of the two day hearing all defendants were found guilty, with Estuary Radio Ltd. being fined £200 and the individual directors £40 each, but this time the station remained on the air pending the outcome of an appeal against this, its second, conviction.

Aggrieved by this apparent defiance of the magistrates' decision the Post Office applied to the High Court seeking an injunction to prevent Radio 390 from continuing to broadcast. David Lye accused the Post Office of trying to prevent the station's appeal by issuing the writ and confirmed that Radio 390 would only cease broadcasting if the High Court granted the injunction.

This case was eventually heard in May when an injunction requiring Radio 390 to cease its transmissions was granted. However, Sir Peter Rawlinson successfully pleaded for a 19 day period of grace while leave was sought to appeal against the decision. David Lye said, "we have lost today, but our fight to keep the station on the air goes on."

Meanwhile, the other remaining Thames Estuary fort-based station, Radio City, was also continuing to broadcast - not yet having been summonsed or prosecuted because the authorities had delayed taking action. This was allegedly because of the outstanding criminal charges involving Major Oliver Smedley, but these had actually been disposed of in October 1966. The more likely reason for the delay was the public statements made by police and other official agencies at the time of the Radio City boarding in June 1966 of 'uncertainty' over the territorial position of Shivering Sands - an excuse they then used for not taking any decisive action against the boarding party.

Eventually the authorities did act and on 31st January a summons was issued against Dorothy Calvert, Radio City's Managing Director, alleging the illegal use of a radio transmitter on Shivering Sands in contravention of the Wireless Telegraphy Act 1949. At Rochford Magistrates Court on 8th February. Mrs. Calvert defended her station's right to broadcast by arguing that all personnel travelling to and from the Fort were subject to clearance by HM Customs and, when Radio City had been forcibly boarded the previous June, police had taken no action because Shivering Sands was considered to be outside their jurisdiction.

But the magistrates were not persuaded by Mrs. Calvert's arguments and ruled that the Fort was within British territorial waters. Mrs. Calvert was fined £100, but no order was made for costs or for the confiscation of Radio City's transmitting equipment. Mrs. Calvert reluctantly decided that the station should close without any undue delay and at 12 midnight on 8th February Radio City left the air for the last time. The final hour was filled with a nostalgic discussion amongst the Radio City DJs about life on the station and the prospects for the future of radio broadcasting in Britain.

In March 1967 yet another offshore radio station found itself in court for allegedly broadcasting within British territorial waters, but unlike previous cases involving the Thames Estuary fort-based stations this time it was the ship-based Radio Scotland. The station had moved during the previous summer to a position off Troon on the west coast of Scotland in an effort to improve its signal to the Glasgow area. It was the choice of anchorage after this move and the application of the Territorial Waters Order in Council of 1964 relating to the definition of what constitutes a bay that led to the prosecution.

The case was heard on 13th March at Ayr Sherriff's Court where the prosecution alleged that "on 14th September 1966 on a hulk moored in the Firth of Clyde, near Lady Isle, in the Parish of Dundonald, in territorial waters adjacent to the British Isles, Radio Scotland had used a transmitter for the purpose of wireless telegraphy without a licence." As with previous cases the Post Office relied on the provisions of the Order in Council relating to the area of water required to define a bay, thus putting the *Comet's* anchorage position within territorial limits.

In Court the Procurator Fiscal said that Post Office engineers had monitored Radio Scotland's broadcasts from three positions on the Ayrshire coast and plotted the position of its vessel, under the terms of the Order in Council, as being at least **35 miles inside** territorial waters. Radio Scotland's solicitor stated that the station's owners had honestly believed that they were operating from international waters as their ship was moored six and a half miles from the nearest coastline.

City and County Commercial Radio (Scotland) Ltd., which pleaded guilty to the charge was fined £80, but a 'not guilty' plea by Managing Director Tommy Shields was accepted by the Court. Following this prosecution the station left the air while preparations were made to tow the *Comet* back to a new anchorage off Scotland's east coast.

Bad weather caused a cancellation of the planned five day tow and the ship was forced to lay silently at anchor off Troon for two weeks with only one DJ and a skeleton crew on board. During gales at the beginning of April the *Comet* broke from her anchor and was only saved from drifting ashore by a tug which towed the radio ship up and down Kames Bay for two days until an emergency anchor could be lowered.

Throughout this period Radio Scotland was off the air and losing an estimated £1,000 each day in advertising revenue, while the cost of keeping the silent radio ship at anchor was put at £1,500 per week. The station's directors decided that something had to be done urgently to put the station back on the air so, on 7th April, the *Comet* was towed to a position off Ballywater, Northern Ireland and from here transmissions were started using the call sign Radio Scotland and Ireland and later Radio 242.

However, the signal in Scotland was weak and problems were encountered with the Irish authorities who insisted that the station's tender should either operate from a Customs port or pay a fee to cover the cost of a Customs officer traveling to another port to inspect goods being taken out to the radio ship. In the end it was decided to run a tender from Belfast (a Customs port) rather than pay the additional fees, but this meant that it had to travel a distance of more than 20 miles to reach the *Comet*.

242 RADIO SCOTLAND'S SHOWBEAT MONTHLY

APRIL. 1966 — Vol. No. 1.

ONE SHILLING

1967. Pier Vick Ltd., the managing company behind Britain Radio and the former Radio England was in severe financial difficulties and went into voluntary liquidation in March with debts of £111,491 and assets of only £5,004.

Complaints were also received that Radio Scotland and Ireland/Radio 242 was causing interference to lighthouse communications in Belfast Lough and to licensed broadcasting services in Ireland. So at the end of April, after just three weeks on the air from its Northern Ireland anchorage, transmissions from the *Comet* were terminated and arrangements were made to tow her back to a position off on the east coast of Scotland. However, due to delays caused by gales and bad weather instead of the planned five days the towing operation took over three weeks, leading to further loss of revenue for the station.

All this time off the air between March and May 1967 had cost Radio Scotland an estimated £15,000 in lost advertising revenue alone. On top of that the station had incurred the cost of towing the *Comet* first to Belfast Lough and then back to the east coast of Scotland. Staffing problems were encountered at the end of May, shortly after the station had returned to the air from its east coast anchorage. Radio Scotland's Co-ordination Controller was blamed for the whole fiasco and sacked, then four DJs (including Senior DJ Bob Spencer), together with the station's Sales and Promotions Manager resigned in sympathy, causing further problems for the station both at sea and on land.

At this time financial projections by the station's accountants showed that in order to recoup its initial investment and cover the annual running costs of £100,000 Radio Scotland would need to remain on the air, in a revenue earning situation, for at least another nine months. The station had resorted to broadcasting an appeal for listeners to make donations towards the cost of moving the *Comet* again after the company's prosecution in March 1967, but despite Radio Scotland's huge audience only £325 was raised.

Problems of a financial nature were also affecting another offshore broadcaster early in

The previous November the former Radio England frequency had been leased to Dutch broadcaster, Radio Dolifjn, but Britain Radio's easy listening format broadcasts had continued despite declining advertising revenue and audience levels.

Britain Radio had set out to challenge 'sweet music' station Radio 390, but their American style format had not worked with British audiences. A number of informal approaches were made by the American team to Ted Allbeury, Managing Director of Radio 390, suggesting either a merger of the two stations or a joint management operation, however, the other Directors of Radio 390 refused to consider these options.

In February 1967 Ted Allbeury had resigned as Managing Director of Radio 390, having been unsuccessful in persuading his fellow directors either to join with Britain Radio on the *Laissez Faire* or to use the former Radio Syd and Caroline South vessel, *Cheeta 2* as a base for the 'sweet music' station.

Shortly after leaving Radio 390 Ted Allbeury was again approached by the management of the now ailing Pier Vick company inviting him to join Britain Radio as Managing Director. Ted Allbeury eventually agreed to look at the American station's financial records and Pier Vick asked for his advice on their continued operation. Based on what he had seen in the financial papers Ted Allbeury's recommendation to the Americans was not to spend any further money on the project because, on anticipated performance, Britain Radio would be unable to turn in a profit before the M.O.B. became law later in the year.

Undeterred by this recommendation the Pier Vick management then asked Ted Allbeury how much it would cost to keep Britain Radio on the air and agreed to put up whatever was required financially if he would agree to run the station. Two days after his resignation from Radio 390 Ted Allbeury joined Britain Radio, announcing in a press interview that " Britain Radio is a very professionally run outfit, they are determined to go on despite the difficulties they have been having."

However, almost as soon as he had been appointed Jack Curtis, the American General Manager of Britain Radio, resigned 'for professional and personal reasons', but it was obvious that the two men had widely differing views about the future format for the easy listening station. Ted Allbeury had plans to introduce the Radio 390 concept of 15 and 30 minute programming segments to Britain Radio - a style which Jack Curtis called "Stone Age Radio, a series of segmented dirges stitched together by sterile announcements." In response Ted Allbeury referred to Britain Radio's existing format, which had been conceived and operated by Jack Curtis, as a "lucky dip".

Before any real format changes could be introduced the weather intervened during the third week of February when the *Laissez Faire's* aerial mast was damaged after the vessel became caught in early spring tides and a Force 9 gale. The storm damage caused the top section of the mast to shear off, bringing with it two cage aerials and a tangle of guy wires. The debris fell over the side of the *Laissez Faire* causing her to take on a 15 degree list. In an attempt to stabalise the vessel the inexperienced crew lashed the wreckage to the side of the *Laissez Faire* and started the engines to try and turn the ship and prevent further damage. The Coastguards, lifeboat service and Air Sea Rescue service were all alerted, but eventually the weather calmed sufficiently for the crew to secure the remaining wreckage of the aerial and prevent further damage to the radio ship.

A few days later the *Laissez Faire's* Captain returned to assess the damage which had been caused to his vessel and, with both radio stations off the air, most DJs from the Dutch and English stations were taken off the ship, leaving just two English DJs and two transmitter engineers on board. On 7th March the Captain was instructed to take the vessel to a ship yard near Amsterdam for repair and on arrival in Holland the Dutch Customs authorities came aboard and sealed the transmitter room and studios.

One of the station's original American backers, Tom Dannaher, visited the radio ship in Zaandam and authorised the shipyard to carry out repairs to the mast. This authorisation to incur expenditure was given at a time when the station's management company, Pier Vick, was in severe financial difficulties and it went into voluntary receivership before repairs could be completed.

The new Managing Director of Britain Radio, Ted Allbeury immediately entered into negotiations with the Receiver and a new company –Carstead Advertising – was formed to take over operation of the twin stations on the *Laissez Faire*. The new owners planned to re-launch Britain Radio as Radio 355, with a format based partly on the successful Radio 390 style, still aiming largely at a 'housewife' audience, but with a more up-tempo range of music.

Radio 355 programme schedule - March 1967

6.00am	Rise and Shine
7.00am	Breakfast Club
9.00am	Double Feature
9.30am	Light and Bright
10.30am	Pause for Prayer
10.40am	Showcase
11.00am	Elevenses
11.30am	Top of the Morning
12.30pm	The World Tomorrow
1.00pm	Requests
2.00pm	Melody Hour
3.00pm	Cafe Continental
3.30pm	Allegro
4.00pm	For the Children
4.15pm	Afternoon Star
4.30pm	Mainly Instrumental
5.30pm	Middle of the Road
6.30pm	The World Tomorrow
7.00pm	Make Mine Country Style
7.30pm	Requests
8.00pm	Music in the Night

Repairs to the *Laissez Faire* were completed and the ship sailed back to her anchorage off the Essex coast at the end of February, starting broadcasts for the new station, Radio 355. For a while the Dutch language station Radio Dolfijn also continued to broadcast from the *Laissez Faire*.

However, the format change introduced on Radio 355 was a cause of dissent amongst the station's staff. A number of ex-Radio 390 announcers had been engaged to join Radio 355 with instructions to introduce the new format, but this did not meet with enthusiasm amongst the former Britain Radio DJs who had rejoined the *Laissez Faire*. Additionally some of the ex-Radio 390 staff experienced problems settling to the way of life aboard a radio ship - they were used to presenting programmes from the relative calm and stability of a sea fort.

After a few weeks of operating the Radio 390 programming style Ted Allbeury realised that it was not going to be as successful as he had hoped and the format was changed back to the original three or four hour 'horizontal' programming style previously used on Britain Radio.

But deep professional frictions now developed between the ex-390 announcers and the former Britain Radio staff who had remained with the ship-based station. After this latest format change some of the ex-390 announcers left and returned to their former station on Red Sands Fort (which was still on the air thanks to the protracted legal appeals waiting to be heard in the courts). Meanwhile, a new team of DJs was recruited for Radio 355.

Fortunately the change in programming style worked and estimates in mid-1967 showed that, despite the station's initial difficulties and its relatively short life-span, Radio 355 had built an audience in the region of 2,250,000, compared with Britain Radio's 718,000 in the NOP Survey twelve months earlier. However, the station still found difficulty in attracting substantial amounts of advertising and relied heavily on sponsored American religious programmes for much of its income.

With the successful re-launch of Radio 355 completed attention was then turned by Ted Allbeury to the re-launch of the Dutch station operating from the *Laissez Faire*. The format

of Radio Dolfijn—easy listening during the daytime and Top 40 at night—was having little impact on Dutch audiences and advertisers, who generally preferred the Top 40 format of Radio Veronica.

So a decision was made to re-launch the Dutch language station as Radio 227, using the former Swinging Radio England pop format and even that station's jingles were canabalised and edited for the new station. Radio 227 was officially launched on 3rd June 1967 and within two weeks was claiming to have attracted audiences far in excess of the level Radio Dolfijn had been able to achieve. However, the new station still could not match the popularity of the well established Radio Veronica and advertising revenue remained low.

The Marine etc. Broadcasting (Offences) Bill was due to receive its Second Reading in the House of Commons during February 1967 and in the weeks prior to this a number of listeners' pressure groups (or 'free radio supporters' as they became more generally known) were established.

First of these groups was the Commercial Radio Listeners Association (CRLA) which was launched at the end of January. Three weeks later, at a meeting in London attended by representatives of many offshore stations, the Free Radio Supporters Association (FRSA) was formed. For their part the radio stations' representatives agreed that they would help the Association in any way they could, short of providing finance or being represented on its governing committee. In practice this meant broadcasting 'commercials' and announcements on behalf of the Association urging listeners to 'join the fight for free radio'.

The CRLA and the FRSA soon merged and, following notification from Ronan O'Rahilly that Radio Caroline would only carry announcements if the word 'supporters' was dropped from its title, the organisation became known as the Free Radio Association (FRA). Announcements for the FRA were broadcast on most of the remaining offshore stations advertising a range of publicity material - car stickers, badges, leaflets etc. and urging listeners to write to their Member of Parliament expressing support for the

fight for FREE RADIO

join us...send s.a.e. for free associate membership

FREE RADIO ASSOCIATION
239 Eastwood road Rayleigh Essex

continuation of the service provided by offshore radio stations.

The Free Radio Association also collected thousands of signatures from supporters for a petition which stated:-

"The Free Radio Association is fighting for free speech, free enterprise and free choice. The Government is trying to crush all competition over the air by silencing the commercial stations - thereby preserving the monopoly of the BBC and depriving us of the freedom to listen to the stations of our choice. This is a step towards dictatorship. If the Marine etc Broadcasting (Offences) Bill becomes law in its present form, free speech will be suppressed, and the Free Radio Association will be partially silenced. No doubt this would please the Government. But the Government will never silence us completely. We have pledged that we will fight and we will win."

Another supporters' organisation which received publicity on the offshore stations was the Broadside Free Radio Movement, formed by a Cambridge University student in April 1967, recruiting initially from the two universities of Oxford and Cambridge. In June the headquarters of the organisation was moved to London and national recruitment began following publicity on Radio Caroline. By July the Movement claimed a membership of 80,000 but by October it had collapsed totally with financial debts of £500. The Free Radio Association

Broadside Free Radio Movement
Mount Street • London W1

membership card

| name |
| number |
| address |

took over the outstanding debts and combined Broadside's membership with its own creating an organisation with a claimed membership of more than 100,000.

Two stations, Radio London and Radio 270, also mounted their own campaigns against the proposed legislation - Radio London DJs constantly requested listeners to 'fight for free radio' by writing to their MPs, while Radio 270 followed a similar pattern and also published, in conjunction with the Institute of Economic Affairs, a booklet entitled *Competition in Radio*, by Denis Thomas. This traced the development of commercial radio abroad as well as in Britain and concluded by supporting the introduction of a legal commercial radio system.

One further voice in support of offshore radio, came with the launch of a national publication devoted to the stations and their programmes,

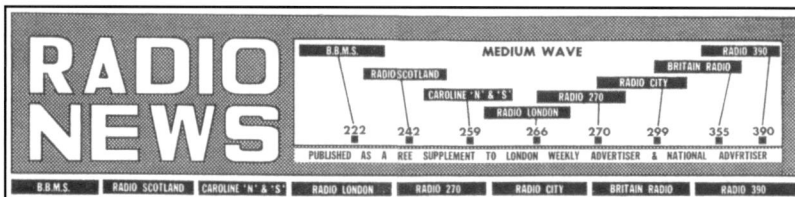

RADIO NEWS

					MEDIUM WAVE				
	B.B.M.S.								RADIO 390
		RADIO SCOTLAND						BRITAIN RADIO	
			CAROLINE 'N' & 'S'				RADIO CITY		
				RADIO LONDON	RADIO 270				
	222	242	259	266	270	299	355	390

PUBLISHED AS A FREE SUPPLEMENT TO LONDON WEEKLY ADVERTISER & NATIONAL ADVERTISER

| B.B.M.S. | RADIO SCOTLAND | CAROLINE 'N' & 'S' | RADIO LONDON | RADIO 270 | RADIO CITY | BRITAIN RADIO | RADIO 390 |

something which had been conspicuous by its absence for nearly three years. In mid-January 1967 a programme listings paper, *Radio News,* was published as a supplement to the *National Advertiser* (a contemporary rival to *Exchange and Mart*) and contained news and articles about the offshore stations, including detailed programme schedules. Editorially the paper argued strongly for the introduction of a legal system of land-based commercial radio in Britain, however, *Radio News* only lasted for nine issues and in March 1967 it was transferred, in a smaller format, to *Time and Tide* magazine where it was eventually phased out due to the impending introduction of legislation banning offshore radio.

Unfortunately all these campaigns, both by the listeners' organisations and the stations themselves came too late to be effective against the Government's legislative plans. The FRA had only achieved a fully paid-up membership of a few thousand by the beginning of June 1967 and as the spring and early summer months passed the stations themselves soon realised the futility of trying to prevent the introduction of legislation, although they continued to broadcast promotions against the M.O.B. and urged listeners to contact their MPs or a member of the House of Lords.

Any supporters of the offshore stations who took the time and trouble to write to their MP, the Postmaster General or even the Prime Minister received the following standard, somewhat patronising reply:-

"Many people have been very disappointed to hear that pirate broadcasting is to be stopped. It seems so harmless and is enjoyed by so many people.

In fact, despite the repeated claims of the pirates, their broadcasts are far from harmless. The pirates are using wavelengths which we have undertaken to leave clear for the broadcasting services in other countries. By so doing they prevent people in those countries from hearing their own domestic programmes. They also represent a danger - slight but ever present- to the radio services on which safety of life at sea depends. Moreover, broadcasting from the high seas is forbidden all over the world by international law. And the pirates make almost unlimited use of recorded material, threatening the livelihoods of the musicians and other performers whose work they use without permission or payment.

To date twelve European countries have complained to the Postmaster General about the pirates' interference with their broadcasting services. And communications between ships and the shore have often been seriously interfered with. If the pirate stations were allowed to continue unchecked there would soon be so much interference that broadcasting as we know it would become impossible.

This threat to the future of broadcasting has caused the maritime countries of the Council of Europe to agree to legislate on common lines to deal with it. The current legislation in this country carries out our obligations under the European Agreement.

Many people feel that an easy solution would be to 'bring the pirates ashore', that is to licence them to operate on land. This is just not possible. There are no unused wavelengths on which powerful stations like the pirate

stations could operate without causing interference. In any case, if they operated within the control of the copyright laws they could not transmit the sort of programmes they have been transmitting.

The Government's plans for the future of sound broadcasting which have recently been announced, are designed to match our broadcasting services more closely to our needs without interfering with other people's rights.

But the most pressing need is to silence the pirate stations, which are flouting international regulations, earning us a bad name abroad, endangering shipping and threatening to make broadcasting end in chaos, not only in Britain but over most of Europe."

The House of Commons debated the Marine etc. Broadcasting (Offences) Bill on 15th February when Labour Postmaster General Edward Short moved the Second Reading. He accused the offshore stations of pirating frequencies not allocated to them under international agreements, of allowing their transmissions to interfere with licensed stations and emergency communications and of being a hazard to shipping. The provisions of the Bill, he said, were intended to make it so difficult for offshore broadcasters to obtain supplies and advertising revenue that they would soon go out of business. If enough other countries enacted similar legislation in accordance with the 1965 Council of Europe agreement (the Strasbourg Convention) then, argued Mr. Short, the stations would have no sources of financial or material supply.

The Conservative (opposition) Spokesman on Broadcasting, Paul Bryan, moved an amendment declining to give the Bill a Second Reading until a comprehensive broadcasting policy had been put in place, taking into account the wishes of millions of listeners, the interests of artists and copyright holders as well as Britain's international radio frequency obligations. The opposition argument centred not specifically on support for offshore radio, but on the need to introduce a replacement service and a wider choice for the listening public which would be commercially funded rather than provided by the BBC out of licence payer's money. A market had been identified by the offshore radio stations, but it was not intended that they should necessarily become the beneficiaries of any new landbased radio structure. However, when it came to the vote the amendments were defeated and the Bill received its Second Reading with a Government majority of 87.

The Bill then passed to the Committee Stage where opposition Conservative MPs proposed a number of further amendments, all of which were defeated:-

- to exempt Scotland from the provisions of the Bill, on the grounds that some of the more remote areas could only receive Radio Scotland's transmissions;

- to exclude the clause relating to offshore television broadcasts;

- to delay the implementation of the Bill for two years after the Royal Assent (and then only with the approval of both Houses of Parliament) to give sufficient time for an alternative radio service to be established.

The result of the Committee Stage deliberations were reported back to the House of Commons early in April. During this Report Stage a further attempt was made to exclude Scotland from the Bill's provisions, as was a proposal to exempt any offshore station which used only VHF (FM) transmissions. A new and potentially significant amendment was also proposed seeking to delete the clause which prevented newspapers publishing programme schedules of the offshore radio stations, effectively gagging the press in its freedom to publish information. Postmaster General Edward Short argued in favour of the Bill's clause, saying that it was a necessary provision which would be used to penalise any publications who collaborated with the stations.

Having completed most of its stages in the House of Commons the Bill then passed to the House of Lords for consideration. Here, on 1st May 1967, an opposition amendment was proposed by Lord Denham seeking to delay implementation of the Bill until alternative programmes had been provided for the 20 million listeners to the offshore radio stations. Lord Denham argued that " it is the Government's responsibility to fill the void left in the lives of their listeners by the planned demise of pirate ships with a satisfactory

alternative. If they don't then someone else will do it for them." For the Government Lord Sorenson stated that the time gap between the demise of the offshore stations and the introduction of a replacement (BBC) service would only be six or seven weeks and that by supporting the amendment the Lords would be "conniving at continued illegality".

When the vote was taken, to the surprise and anger of the Government, the amendment was carried with an opposition majority of 21. This success was short-lived, however, because when the Bill completed its parliamentary progress during the Third (and final) Reading in the Commons on 30th June the Lord's amendment was reversed. The Bill now only required the Royal Assent to become law.

As the Parliamentary process continued the stations themselves came to realise that arguments about freedom of expression and rights of democracy would have little impact on the Government   and, despite the fleeting success of the Lord's amendment, the Bill to outlaw them was almost certain to become law before the end of the summer. Consequently, feeling that they had nothing more to lose, some offshore stations gradually became involved in politics in various ways - something which they had all previously avoided.

During March and April 1967 Radio London commissioned a survey of candidates in the Greater London Council (GLC) elections to establish who supported or opposed the offshore stations. The results, which were repeatedly broadcast by Radio 270 and Radio Caroline as well as Radio London itself showed the following breakdown of candidates' views :-

	FOR	AGAINST	DON'T KNOW
Labour	4	23	1
Liberal	28	6	0
Conservative	38	0	0

An opinion poll of MPs was also conducted at the same time and this showed, not surprisingly, that the majority of the (Labour) Government's MPs wanted the stations to be closed, while 65% of opposition (Conservative) MPs were in favour of the service provided by offshore radio.

In Yorkshire, Radio 270 agreed to accept advertisements from political parties for candidates standing in the local council elections when the Young Conservatives at York University bought air time. A further party political broadcast by York University Conservative Association was transmitted over Radio 270 in June.

With the passing of the Marine etc. Broadcasting (Offences) Bill by Parliament on 30th June the offshore stations knew that they would either have to close or make elaborate alternative financial and staffing arrangements to circumvent the legislation and stay on the air.

Some stations had already begun to make alternative arrangements earlier in the year in case their efforts to defeat the legislation

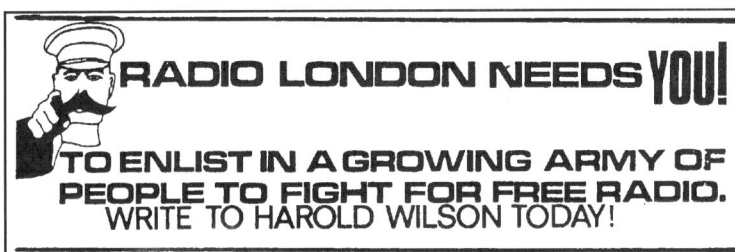
RADIO LONDON NEEDS YOU! TO ENLIST IN A GROWING ARMY OF PEOPLE TO FIGHT FOR FREE RADIO. WRITE TO HAROLD WILSON TODAY!

failed. In January Radio Caroline staff took over the Roughs Tower off Felixstowe, which was outside British jurisdiction, even taking into account the provisions of the 1964 Order in Council for calculating territorial limits, which had been used as the main argument in the successful prosecutions against the fort-based stations and Radio Scotland. Radio Caroline's personnel removed much of the wartime superstructure and created a helicopter landing pad on the Fort's platform.

The station intended using the Fort as a supply and accommodation base for servicing the Caroline South ship, enabling food and fuel to be stockpiled there for later transfer to the radio ship without directly contravening the Marine etc. Broadcasting (Offences) Act.

However, another offshore radio station operator also had plans for Roughs Tower. After his prosecution and conviction in January 1967 Roy Bates decided to move the Radio Essex/BBMS transmitting equipment from Knock John Fort to Roughs Tower and there were a number of violent disputes

between the two groups. An agreement was eventually reached that both Radio Caroline and Roy Bates would share occupation of Roughs Tower and accordingly each group landed two men on the Fort. The uneasy peace lasted for a few weeks until April when Bates's group took total possession of Roughs Tower while the Radio Caroline men had to go ashore for one of them to receive medical treatment.

The Radio Caroline organisation made a number of attempts to regain a hold on the Fort but were constantly repelled. This rivalry came to a violent head on 27th June when Radio Caroline sent a boarding party in an attempt to finally reclaim possession of Roughs Tower, but as the Caroline party tried to climb onto the Fort Roy Bates's men opened fire on them with petrol bombs and guns.

Ronan O'Rahilly said he had plans for the Fort which were nothing to do with broadcasting, claiming it was to be developed as a health centre and holiday hotel. Roy Bates also claimed the Fort was his and although the Radio Essex equipment was on board he did not intend to set up a radio station. "We intend to stay here against all comers" said Mr. Bates, backing up his claim by showing reporters the armoury of weapons held on the Fort, including six shotguns, a flame thrower, two air rifles and a supply of petrol bombs.

Although Essex Police met the Radio Caroline party when they returned to port and took statements from them no action was taken over the incident because Roughs Tower was indeed outside British territorial limits and the police genuinely had no powers to act against either party.

April Fool Hoax

On 1st April 1967 some DJs and engineers on Radio London played an April Fool's hoax on listeners. Normal Radio London programmes were 'interrupted' by a 'new' station calling itself Radio East Anglia, between 9.30am and 11.55am. Hundreds of listeners even telephoned the Post Office to complain about the 'new' station affecting reception of Radio London.

SEALAND

Roy Bates having established physical control of Roughs Tower set about creating his own sovereign territory on the Fort. On 20th September 1967 he declared it to be the independent Principality of Sealand with himself as Prince Roy and his wife as Princess Joan. A red, white and black flag was raised on the Fort to demonstrate its independent status and the new state issued its own passports, currency and postage stamps.

Unfortunately for Roy Bates few of these initiatives were recognised by the international community, although the Belgian Post Office delivered letters bearing the Sealand stamps and France and Spain accepted Sealand passports as proof of identity. The coinage only remained legal tender on the Principality itself although it was of interest to collectors, as were the postage stamps.

The British Government refused to accept Sealand as an independent state because it did not fulfil the conditions required for statehood under international law. However, Dr. Pela Vitanyi, a professor of international law at Nijmegen University in Holland advised Roy Bates that he had effectively taken control of territory without a master and because the British authorities had not acted against him they had effectively accepted his claim to the Fort.

Roy Bate's claim to sovereignty seemed to be reinforced by a British court in 1968 when his son, Michael, was charged with illegal possession of firearms and firing shots at Trinity House personnel. The Court ruled that it could not hear the case because Roughs Tower (Sealand) lay outside British territorial limits. A further boost to the independent status of Sealand came in May 1979 when the Archbishop of Canterbury gave permission for a wedding to be conducted on the Fort. Gordon Wilkinson, Sealand's Security Chief, married Karen Huxtable in a ceremony conducted by the vicar of Harwich, Rev. Jim Chelton.

Over the years Sealand has been rumoured to be planning the launch of radio and television services - plans for three stations in the mid-1970s, and Arabic station in 1980, satellite radio relays in 1983 and Sealand TV in 1986, but all came to nothing. A group of amateur radio operators from Germany did, however, transmit on shortwave and FM from Sealand in September 1983 and were given special Sealand call-signs for the month long duration of their broadcasts.

A number of elaborate plans for the development of Sealand have been made, including the construction of floating hotels, leisure complexes and the creation of a freeport, but all have come to nothing. The introduction of the British Territorial Sea Act 1987 effectively brought Roughs Tower inside British territorial limits and all chance of independent developments taking place seemed to fade.

Despite this decision by the police Roy Bates later revealed that the Ministry of Defence had offered to pay him £5,000 to return the structure to the Crown. A detachment of Royal Marines and two helicopters were actually put on stand-by in case negotiations with Bates were successful, so that the Fort could be quickly reclaimed and anyone else - in particular Radio Caroline - prevented from taking possession of it again. Roy Bates, however, refused the offer from the Ministry of Defence and retained possession of Roughs Tower, eventually declaring it to be an 'independent state' - Sealand on 20th September 1967.

During the time Radio Caroline had been in partial possession of Roughs Tower, in March, the station also asked 20 of its British staff to consider giving up their citizenship if they wished to remain employed after the M.O.B. became law. The station also engaged seven more American and Canadian staff to enable it to continue broadcasting and made arrangements with a French public relations firm, to secure advertising from European sources. Meanwhile Terry Bate, who had joined Radio Caroline in 1966 to improve its sales operation, used his company in Toronto to try and secure advertising for the station from businesses in North America. An office was also opened in Holland in May to act as the new headquarters after the British legislation came into effect. Plans were also announced to secure further income by launching a second service from the *Mi Amigo* in addition to Radio Caroline South, to be staffed by Dutch DJs with programmes directed at Holland, tapping into the lucrative Dutch advertising market.

Carstead Advertising, operators of Radios 355 and 227, also opened an office in Amsterdam with the object of trying to secure foreign advertising to enable the twin stations to continue broadcasting after the new British legislation became law.

At the end of May 1967 three transmitter valves were delivered to the Radio London vessel *Galaxy*, so that, from a technical point of view, the station would be able to continue broadcasting for anything up to six years. The station also set up an office in Holland to act as a supply base and Managing Director Philip Birch announced that in future Radio London would rely almost entirely on American advertising income.

Tendering arrangements for the larger stations were made through the Offshore Supply Company, a subsidiary of the Dutch salvage organisation Wijsmuller. Directors of the Dutch company informed the offshore stations that their vessels, *Offshore I, II,* and *III* would still be available for tendering purposes after the new British legislation had been introduced, but they would have to operate from bases in Holland, Spain, or Ireland rather than south east England or the Isle of Man.

Early in July Radio Caroline announced that on the first day the new legislation came into effect the station would use a British DJ, newsreader and religious broadcaster to break the law by taking part in programmes. Ronan O'Rahilly threatened to challenge any

subsequent prosecution of these British staff at the Court of Human Rights in Strasbourg, although legal experts had considerable doubts as to whether such action would have been successful.

Poet, dramatist and founder of the English Stage Company, Ronald Duncan also announced in the *Daily Telegraph* on 23rd June 1967 that he had offered his services to Radio Caroline after the new legislation had become effective. He had already written a series of brief sketches pointing out the likely effects, in terms of freedom of speech and freedom of the individual, of the provisions contained in the M.O.B. and these had been broadcast on Radio Caroline since the spring of 1967. Ronald Duncan called on other writers to join him because, he said, "This is an issue of far greater importance than at first appears. Its implications cut right across the freedoms of the individual. As has been proved so often in history these can be easily whittled away - and when they are it takes a formidable social upheaval to re-establish them."

The Marine etc. Broadcasting (Offences) Act received the Royal Assent on 14th July 1967 and Postmaster General Edward Short announced that its provisions would come into effect one month later, on 15th August. One by one the offshore stations gave their reactions to this news. With the reality of the legislation becoming law and despite earlier defiant claims to the contrary, Radios 270, Scotland, 355 and 227 all announced that they would close before the 15th August deadline.

Radio 390 was, at that time, still fighting its own appeal against prosecution under entirely different legislation, but the directors had already rejected transferring operations from the Red Sands Fort to a ship in international waters so the outlook for the station was not very optimistic. Only the two largest stations, Radio London and Radio Caroline, confirmed that they would definitely continue broadcasting after 15th August. Philip Birch of Radio London made one final desperate plea to the Postmaster General calling on him to "allow the stations to continue supplying 25 million listeners with a popular music service which they have enjoyed for the past three years."

Radio London programme schedule - June 1967	
5.00am	Pete Drummond
9.00am	Paul Kaye
11.00am	Coffee Break
12noon	Tony Brandon
3.00pm	Mark Roman
6.00pm	Pete Drummond
7.00pm	The World Tomorrow
7.30pm	Pete Drummond
9.00pm	Willy Walker
12midnight	John Peel

Radio 390's application to be allowed to continue broadcasting on the grounds that the Red Sands Fort was outside territorial limits was finally heard in the Court of Appeal in July 1967. Judgement was given, ruling that the Fort was definitely within territorial limits and dismissing the station's appeal against its February conviction. Counsel for Estuary Radio Ltd asked for a stay to enable the station to remain on the air until the Marine etc. Broadcasting (Offences) Act (M.O.A.) came into effect on 15th August, but the Court refused this application. Lord Justice Sellars told the defendants "There is no reason why you should broadcast any longer, all you have to do is cease broadcasting 18 days earlier than you would have done."

After the hearing David Lye, Acting Managing Director of Estuary Radio Ltd., told reporters that the protracted legal battle had cost the station £10,000 and as a consequence the company had lost virtually all the profit it had earned over the year and ten months Radio 390 had been broadcasting.

Because no direct communication between the station's land-based office and the Fort was permitted Radio 390 staff listened to the BBC 1.00pm news bulletin to hear of the Appeal Court's decision. Radio 390 programmes continued as normal throughout the afternoon of 28th July until official instructions were received from the station's management.

Arrangements were made for a tender to be despatched from Whitstable for the last time carrying instructions for staff on the Fort to cease transmissions and finally close Radio 390. The tender arrived at Red Sands shortly after the station's 5.00pm news had been read and the next programme, "On the Scene" was started by announcer Christopher Clark. After the end of the first record senior announcer Edward Cole interrupted the programme to read the message which had been sent from the management of Estuary Radio Ltd.:-

'Due to an injunction imposed in the High Court today, at the request of the Post Office, Radio 390 is now required to cease broadcasting. We should like to express our immense appreciation to the millions of listeners who have always supported us during the past two years and through our many struggles to stay on the air. It is very disappointing to all of us that we are not able to continue to provide you with the programmes you enjoy, but perhaps one day we will be allowed to do so again. Until then on behalf of Mr. Lye, our London office, the relief staff and everybody here I should like to say goodbye.'

At 5.10pm the station played the National Anthem and Radio 390 finally closed.

At the end of July 1967 the BBC unveiled its long awaited plans for the introduction of a pop radio service to replace the offshore stations. The old Home, Light and Third Programme networks were to be abolished and in their place four new stations were to be launched:-

Radio One was the new pop music station.
Radio Two a revamped Light Programme.
Radio Three a classical music and speech channel, replacing the Third Programme.
Radio Four was to carry the Home Service speech and news programmes.

It was claimed that 60 hours a week of extra broadcasting would result from the sweeping changes to be introduced at the end of September 1967.

Radio Caroline programme schedules - June 1967

	Caroline South		*Caroline North*
6.00am	Tommy Vance		Leighton Early Show, Jerry Leighton
9.00am	Mike Ahearn		The Big Wide Wonderful World of 'Daffy' Don Allen
12noon	Dave Lee Travis		Bob Stewart Show
3.00pm	Keith Hampshire		Mick Luvzit
6.00pm	Robbie Dale		Requests in Action
8.30pm	Christ to the Nation	**(8.00)**	The World Tomorrow
9.00pm	Johnnie Walker	**(8.30)**	Closedown
12midnight	Steve Young		Midnight Surf Party

Arguments against and in support of the offshore stations

Despite their huge audience figures the British offshore stations were not popular with everyone, particularly Government departments and various trade organisations - perceived by the former as a threat to existing national and international agreements and by the latter to the vested interests of their own membership.

Many arguments were put forward for outlawing the offshore stations, but essentially they followed variations of one or more of these themes:-

1. The offshore stations 'pirated' frequencies and transmitter powers not allocated to them under international agreements, in particular the 1948 Copenhagen Convention and (occasionally) caused interference to legitimate stations using these frequencies. Britain was a signatory to various international agreements and it was therefore the Government's responsibility to uphold its obligations. As a supplementary to this the international frequency allocation argument was also used to refute any suggestion that the offshore stations should be invited on land or that a network of commercial stations could be established to compete with the BBC. "The frequencies are not available for use in Britain" was the standard reply to any proposals by 'commercial' or 'local' radio pressure groups to establish stations on land.

2. The offshore stations' transmissions interfered with maritime, ship-to-shore and emergency service communications, posing a possible threat to the lives of those who found themselves in distress at sea and needing assistance.

3. The offshore stations avoided paying copyright fees for the recorded music they broadcast and did not observe any 'needletime' restrictions on the number of hours of such music transmitted each week - as the BBC was obliged to do under a hard won agreement with Phonographic Performances Ltd.

As a counter to these accusations the offshore stations, and their supporters, put forward the following arguments:

1. At the time (the mid 1960s) over 300 of the 500 medium wave stations operating in Europe did so on frequencies not allocated under the 1948 Copenhagen Convention, including 'respectable' stations such as Vatican Radio, Voice of America and Radio Luxembourg.

2. Admittedly there had been some complaints of interference in the early days of offshore broadcasting, but the number of instances where offshore transmissions had caused interference with maritime and emergency communications was rare. The offshore stations had a responsibility to avoid such interference being caused by their transmissions, a responsibility which most stations acknowledged. They continually made efforts to avoid providing grounds for any such accusations being directed at them. Apart from this moral responsibility the stations also had a vested interest in avoiding disruption to the emergency service's communications network because they themselves were at some stage likely to need assistance - a fact demonstrated many times during the history of offshore broadcasting.

3. Some of the larger offshore stations offered to make payments for copyright and performance fees (although it must be said the majority did not). Phonographic Performances Ltd. refused to accept any such monies but the Performing Rights Society did accept payments (in particular from Radio Caroline, Radio London and Radio 390) and this fact was much publicised by the stations as evidence of their good intentions. However, what was not so widely publicised by either party was that whilst the PRS openly accepted these payments, the organisation did not feel it could fully condone or support the existence of offshore radio.

With the possible exception of the argument about interference to maritime and emergency communications (which in reality was more of a theoretical than real possibility) the other arguments appear even more irrelevant today than they were forty years ago. Britain now has over 260 commercial local or regional radio stations, 56 BBC local and regional stations, 5 BBC national radio networks and 3 national commercial radio stations, all of whom have been found and allocated frequencies from within Britain's quota under international agreement. Virtually all of these stations have a music based format, pouring out hundreds of hours a week of recorded music. This, it was argued at the height of the offshore stations' popularity, would destroy the music industry and with it the livelihoods of musicians everywhere. Experience has shown that if anything the reverse has proved to be the case.

The offshore radio stations are sometimes remembered as much for the commercials as the music they played. To attract new advertisers they mounted their own campaigns and here is a selection of adverts placed by the offshore stations in the trade press during the 1960's

FOR SALE

10,330,000 PEOPLE

including
8,390,000 Adults*
and
3,640,000 Housewives*
*Source: NOP Survey March 1966

in quantity lots at
Less than 6d per thousand

Available only from 266m

Radio London

Every day-Britain's biggest Commercial
Radio audience

Full details - and a copy of the NOP Survey from
Radlon (Sales) Ltd., 17 Curzon Street London W
MAYfair 5361

'Here are 21
of Carolines' 6,480,000 Housewives Ears

6,480,000 is a lot, particularly when attached to the 3,240,000 housewives who listen to Caroline across the week (N.O.P.) AND REMEMBER 72% OF ALL THE HOUSEWIVES WHO LISTEN TO DAYTIME COMMERCIAL RADIO LISTEN TO RADIO CAROLINE. Want to know more contact Michael Parkin or Murray Robb ... HYD 9721.

Radio Caroline

POP isn't everybody's cup of tea!

And 'Pop' would be the first to agree. He thinks Tom Jones is the name of an opera, and a 'beatle' to him, is something to be kept out of his floor joists. He's not as interested in 'Groups' as he is in greenhouse heating. Pop likes listening to radio as much as anyone else. He likes a good tune, or a talk on gardening, and, like the rest of us, he can't resist a bargain. His choice of listening is 270, because of the balanced programme, with something to interest everybody. Consequently, an ad. for liniment has as much impact as one for lipstick, and we sell as much baccy as bathsalts. We broadcast some 'pop' for the kids, but there's also something for Pop, - and Mum, too.

Send now for rates and programme details.

RADIO 270
(Advertising Sales) LT
ALBEMARLE CHAMBERS
ALBEMARLE CRESCENT
SCARBOROUGH, YORK
Telephone:
Scarborough 83645

LONDON SALES MANAGER
Noel Ranken
50 CANNON STREET
LONDON E.C.4
Telephone: CENTral 6825

Radio 390 gets the message home

(that's where the housewife is)

3:0
Ring Ranken · VIC 0412

Three hundred and ninety good reasons for Radio 390

(Now North and South)

Good reason No. 1. RADIO 390 NORTH, now transmitting off the Wirral Peninsula, adds 17,000,000 people to the 26,000,000 covered in the original RADIO 390 SOUTH area. This gives a potential audience of 79.7% of the total population of Great Britain.
Good reason No. 2. A recent independent electronic survey into signal strength in the Southern coverage area showed that in 99 out of 112 towns where tests were carried out RADIO 390's reception was stronger than that of its main commercial competitor. In 2 other towns the results were equal. Proof positive of real potential in terms of density as well as breadth of coverage.
Good reason No. 3. RADIO 390 SOUTH has installed an FM transmitter that from August 1st will simultaneously transmit the whole of RADIO 390 SOUTH programmes. RADIO 390 SOUTH will be the only off-shore programme available on an extensive 2,000,000 FM receivers in the RADIO 390 SOUTH area. All bonus listeners!
Good reason No. 4. RADIO 390 is proud of its claim —"the sweet music station". Comments from listeners confirm that there is a large number of discriminating people that prefer this kind of music to non-stop pop.
Good reason No. 5. RADIO 390 is the station to reach the over 30's — the mothers and those shopping for their families — the lucrative family purchase market.
If you think you need Good Reasons numbers 6 — 390 why Radio 390 should be on your Advertising Schedule, contact:
Noel Ranken, Sales Controller, Radio 390 (Sales) Ltd., 30A Rathbone Place, London, S.W.1. Tel. Victoria 0412/0413.

3:0

MOTORISTS' EARS:
Over 3½ million adults in car owning families (of which 1¾ million are petrol buyers) listened to Radio Caroline on an average week day.

HOUSEWIVES' EARS:
Over 4½ million housewives listened to Radio Caroline, at some time on Mondays to Fridays, and nearly 5 million on Saturdays and Sundays.

EARS AT WORK:
Over ¼ million adults listened to Radio Caroline between 10 am and 3.00 pm at work, on Mondays to Fridays. Mind you, over 3 million people were listening at home during the same time.

SUNDAY EARS:
Nearly 4½ million people listened to Radio Caroline on Sunday, between 12 noon and 3.00 pm.

TOTAL EARS:
Over 12½ million people listened to Radio Caroline at some time during the week.

Assorted Ears for sale

Matched pairs of ears are available in large lots from Radio Caroline—starting at the unbelievably low price of 5d. per 1,000. Want some? Get them from Michael Parkin Caroline Sales, Caroline House, Chesterfield Gardens, London, W.1. (HYDe Park 9721) Attwood Statistics was the source of the information in this advertisement.

Radio Caroline

Chapter 9   Scuppered!

The same day on which Radio 390 closed, 28th July 1967, Radio London listeners were told in a dramatic announcement that, contrary to previous statements, the station would not continue broadcasting after 15th August. Managing Director Philip Birch said "We have received hundreds of thousands of letters from listeners asking us to continue, but we would be getting too close to the law. As we have never yet broken the law we have decided to cease broadcasting. Our ship will be up for sale." The real reason for the station's closure was, of course, its inability to obtain sufficient advertising revenue from foreign sources to finance continued broadcasting.

A similar problem also affected Carstead Advertising, whose Managing Director Ted Allbeury, had announced earlier in the month that Radios 355 and 227 would also be closing before the Marine etc. Broadcasting (Offences) Act came into effect. Efforts had been made, using Radio 227's office in Holland, to obtain foreign advertising for the two stations, but as with Radio London this had proved unsuccessful.

Dutch language Radio 227 was the first station to close in advance of the new law coming into effect, the station closed without ceremony following the end of normal programmes on 23rd July. Two weeks later Radio 355 closed at midnight on Saturday 5th August.

The station's final two hours were hosted by Programme Director Tony Windsor and all DJs who were on board the *Laissez Faire* at the time also took part. Shortly before midnight the last commercial - for Silexene paint - was played and Managing Director Ted Allbeury made a closing speech pointing out to listeners the restrictions on personal liberty and freedom contained in the M.O.A. Both of the stations operated by Carstead Advertising had closed earlier than necessary because insurance for the *Laissez Faire* had expired and it was not worthwhile extending cover for less than two weeks.

Radio 270's Managing Director, Wilf Proudfoot, announced that the station would close at one minute to midnight on 14th

August, saying "we have not broken the law up to now and we don't intend to in the future." Even before Radio 270's closure the station's vessel *Oceaan VII* was put up for sale through a local firm of estate agents, Tuckley and Co., with an asking price of £25,000.

These closures and announcements of intended closure left Radio Caroline alone in saying it would defy the new law and continue broadcasting after 15th August. Contingency plans for this to happen had already been put in place by the station's management. In June all British members of Radio Caroline's board of directors resigned, except Philip Solomon, who also held Irish citizenship and was therefore able to continue running the station with fellow countryman Ronan O'Rahilly. A number of American, Australian, Canadian and South African DJs were said to have been recruited and standing by to join the station after 15th August. Meanwhile, during the early days of August 1967 on both the North and South stations many British DJs were saying that they would stay on with Radio Caroline and defy the new law.

One demonstration of support for Radio Caroline came unexpectedly from a source that had initially been very hostile to the station - the Isle of Man. The arrival of the MV *Caroline* in July 1964 was seen as a powerful threat to the Island's own local commercial station, but since then Radio Caroline North had become very popular on the Island. This was not just because of the entertainment it provided, but because the station gave the Island's holiday resorts an immense amount of free publicity across a huge listening area, greatly boosting the Manx tourist trade and general economy.

In April 1967, as the British House of Commons was approving the M.O.B., the Isle of Man Parliament, the House of Keys, voted overwhelmingly to reject the same Bill being added to the Island's statute book, and in doing so offered some hope for the future existence of Caroline North. Ronan O'Rahilly even announced that he was negotiating with the Manx authorities to bring Radio Caroline ashore so that the station could operate from a

Support for Caroline North remaining at anchor off the Island was stepped up in July when the Postmaster General rejected a request from the Manx Broadcasting Commission for an increase in transmitter power for the local (legal) commercial station, Manx Radio. If they could not have a powerful station of their own to broadcast the Island's attractions to listeners on the mainland then many Manxmen were happy to see Caroline North remain in Ramsey Bay and to let it fulfill that role for them.

base on the Island, although realistically this was unlikely to have been achieved at that time.

Throughout the summer of 1967, as the British Government proceeded with enacting its own legislation, the Manx Government stood its rebellious ground. Undeterred, Westminster announced at the beginning of August that the M.O.A. would be applied to the Island (and also the Channel Islands) by means of Orders in Council signed by the Queen - effectively imposing the legislation against the wishes of the Island's own Parliament and its people. The prospect of this unwanted piece of legislation being forced on the Island's statute book brought Manx nationalistic feelings to the surface and there was talk of the Island breaking its ties with Westminster and declaring complete independence.

A Member of the House of Keys, Roy McDonald (who was also Chairman of the Manx Broadcasting Commission) proposed a resolution rejecting the imposition of legislation on the Island and demanded that the situation be considered by the United Nations Committee responsible for overseeing the interests of colonial peoples. Roy McDonald emphasised that he was not particularly supporting Radio Caroline, that just happened to have brought the real issue to light. The real issue so far as he and others were concerned was the imposition of unwanted British legislation which had already been rejected by the semi-independent Island's own Parliament. Mr. McDonald's resolution was approved by the House of Keys and the Island's Governor, Sir Peter Stallard, was forced to recall the full Island Parliament, Tynwald, from its summer recess to consider the rapidly deteriorating constitutional situation.

On 3rd August it was announced that Tynwald's petition to the Privy Council had been rejected and, as a consequence, the Queen would be asked to sign an Order in Council imposing the legislation on the Island. After this announcement there was speculation about the Island engaging in all sorts of rebellious activity - the issuing of Manx passports, a takeover of the Post Office service on the Island, and even the creation of a Manx national army, but all came to nothing.

Tynwald, the Manx Parliament, met on 8th August in a joint session of its two Houses - the House of Keys and the Legislative Council. During seven hours of heated debate Roy McDonald agreed to withdraw that part of his resolution referring the imposition of British legislation on the Island to the United Nations, but replaced it with a reference to the Commonwealth Secretariat.

When it came to the vote, the lower house, the House of Keys, supported Roy McDonald's amended resolution by 16 votes to 8, but the upper house, the Legislative Council, voted unanimously against it. The House of Keys immediately adjourned to its own chamber and voted to continue with its previous decision to fight the imposition of unwanted mainland legislation. Ronan O'Rahilly who had witnessed the debate from the public gallery told waiting reporters afterwards that Radio Caroline North would remain in Ramsey Bay whatever the Manx or British Governments decided, any prosecutions of staff or advertisers which arose as a consequence would, he said, be fought all the way to the European Court of Human Rights

The first station to close on Monday 14th August 1967, the day before the M.O.A. came into effect, was Radio London. Throughout the day farewell messages were broadcast from many pop stars who, in part, owed their success to Radio London - Beatle Ringo Starr, The Bee Gees, Cilla Black, Dave Davies, Episode Six, Chris Farlowe, David Garrick, The Hollies, Englebert Humperdink, Tom Jones, The Kinks, Lulu, Sandie Shaw, Nancy Sinatra, The Small Faces, John Walker and several American stars who recorded on the Tamla Mowtown label. During the station's final hour Managing Director Philip Birch told listeners:-

'...If during the last three years Radio London has brought a little warmth, a little friendliness, a little happiness in your life then it's all been worthwhile. As one listener put it "The world will get by without Big L, but I'm not sure if it will be a better place. Thank you.'

The final hour on Radio London had been pre-recorded a few days earlier with the station's last news bulletin at 2.30pm being the only live input. The programme was hosted by senior DJ Paul Kaye and consisted of a brief history of the station, farewell messages from pop stars and DJs as well as some nostalgic music. Advertisers paid heavy premiums for their announcements to be included in this programme - in fact advertising time had been sold at premium rates throughout the station's last few days on the air - and the final commercial broadcast was for Consulate cigarettes. It was estimated that during its relatively short life-span of two years and eight months Radio London had made a £100,000 profit for its investors.

Paul Kaye was the last remaining DJ from the station's original line-up and his was the first and last voice heard on Radio London. After the final record, "A Day in the Life" by the Beatles, had been played Paul Kaye said simply "Big L time is 3 o'clock and Radio London is now closing down". The station left the air after playing its theme music (Big Lil) and one final jingle. Engineers then shut off the transmitter, removed the crystal, switched off the control panel and locked the studio. On Radio Caroline South just after 3.00pm Robbie Dale paid a tribute to the rival station which had just closed. He observed a minute's silence before Radio Caroline returned to playing music - once more the lone voice of offshore radio - in the south at least.

The Big L DJs and radio engineers left the *Galaxy* later that afternoon and were taken to Felixstowe where they were greeted by fans who had gathered on the quayside. This welcome, however, was nothing compared to that which awaited them when their train arrived at Liverpool Street Station in London. Here over 1,000 supporters had gathered during the afternoon and, when the train carrying the Radio London DJs arrived, the crowd surged through barriers and police lines. Hundreds of fans besieged the DJs on the train and many young people as well as the police who were trying to restrain them were knocked down and injured in the crush. When the Radio London staff eventually managed to make their escape from the train to a waiting car this too was surrounded by fans, many of whom climbed on the roof and bonnet.

Meanwhile, the *Galaxy* remained silently at anchor off the Essex coast for a few days with only her Dutch Captain and crew on board, then on 19th August she raised her anchor and sailed to Hamburg. There were many rumours and plans for the ship to be used as an offshore radio station again, but that story unfolded very slowly over the following few years.

In the north two of the three remaining offshore stations also closed shortly before midnight on 14th August 1967.

Off the east coast Radio 270 planned a final hour which was to have included all the station's DJs broadcasting live from on board the *Oceaan VII*. However, rough weather prevented many DJs on shore leave traveling to the ship to join their colleagues but unofficial arrangements were made for a helicopter to drop a tape containing their farewell messages onto the deck of the *Oceaan VII*. This arrangement was made by Radio 270's Deputy Programme Director, Mike Hayes who persuaded a friend at RAF Leconfield to take the tape on a helicopter 'training flight' over the North Sea. Because of the unofficial and unauthorised nature of the delivery the tape was accompanied by a message instructing those on board the *Oceaan VII* not to mention on the air how it had arrived.

Unfortunately when the tape and accompanying message were dropped from the helicopter they landed, not on the deck of the *Oceaan VII* as planned, but in the sea. DJs on board the radio ship, not knowing of the secretive nature of the mission, announced to listeners that an RAF helicopter was hovering over the *Oceaan VII* and thanked "the boys at Leconfield" for coming out to see them on their final day! The RAF authorities immediately launched an official inquiry into this completely unauthorised 'training flight' and it was reported that Prime Minister, Harold Wilson demanded to see a personal copy of the report on the incident.

Radio 270's final hour then went ahead with those DJs who were on board *Oceaan VII*, as well as the Captain and crew reminiscing about life on the station. Unfortunately studio equipment during that final programme suffered from surges in power due to the ship's continuing problem with jelly fish which were being sucked into the generator cooling system, slowing records and distorting the sound quality. At 11.55pm the final announcement was made by Programme Director Vince 'Rusty' Allen and, after playing the National Anthem, the station left the air for the final time at 11.59pm.

From a business point of view Radio 270, which claimed an audience of four and a half million listeners, was not an outstanding success. At one point it had debts of over £50,000, but before the station closed the directors made arrangements for all staff and creditors to be paid out of their own funds so ultimately, the original shareholders were the people who lost financially because of the station's closure.

The DJs and crew who had been on board the *Oceaan VII* left the ship immediately after the station closed and arrived in Bridlington Harbour an hour later where they were met on the quayside by a crowd of about 600 fans. The *Oceaan VII* itself, which had already been offered for sale by local estate agents sailed to Whitby where she was berthed, but the ship and her radio equipment's connections with offshore radio were not finished yet!

Further north, off the Scottish coast, Radio Scotland also closed at midnight on 14th August 1967. The final day's programmes were pre-recorded in the station's Glasgow studios and most of the DJs had already left the *Comet* during the afternoon of 14th August to join 2,000 fans at a Close-down Clan Ball in Glasgow. Mark Wesley and Tony Allan stayed on board the radio ship to play the taped programmes and finally close Radio Scotland.

The station's final hour contained messages and tributes from former staff and from Managing Director, Tommy Shields, who said it was the saddest day of his life. Radio Scotland announced that during the nineteen months it had been on the air the station had lost £100,000, due largely to the cost of towing the *Comet* from the east to the west coast and back again, as well as the general lack of advertising revenue as a result of poor signal quality and frequent periods off the air while the ship was being repositioned.

After spending three days at anchor the *Comet* was eventually towed into the port of Methil, where the aerial mast was removed and the vessel put up for sale.

So, with Tuesday 15th August 1967 less than a minute old only two British offshore radio stations remained on the air in defiance of the new law - Radio Caroline North and Radio Caroline South. On board the *Mi Amigo*, home of Radio Caroline South were three Englishmen - DJs Johnnie Walker and Robbie Dale as well as newsreader Ross Brown.

During the previous day the rest of the British staff had left the *Mi Amigo* for the final time, rather than become exiled from Britain, but by continuing to broadcast the three Englishmen still on board each now faced up to two years in prison and a £400 fine if they ever returned to Britain.

At 12 midnight Johnnie Walker and Robbie Dale, sounding almost as if they were reassuring eachother as much as the listeners, announced that the station, now renamed Caroline International, would continue broadcasting:-

Johnnie Walker *This is your radio station. This is Radio Caroline. It is now 12 midnight. We want to say welcome to the new phase of broadcasting from Caroline. I want you to know something, that is a station that belongs to you and as a right can't ever be taken away* *from you. There are a lot of people along the coast tonight who are flashing their headlamps at us. Very nice to see you. You have made us more happy, and I couldn't think it was possible, but you have made us more happy than we are already. Dale, what are you doing there?*

Robbie Dale *I'm looking out of the porthole window. It really is amazing to see all those cars out there and to know that we're not alone in this our most important moment. It's tremendous!*

Johnnie Walker *Let's say a couple of Thank You's now. Robbie and myself would like to say thank you to our leader, Ronan O'Rahilly, Mr. Philip Soloman and all who work for Radio Caroline to make it possible for us to sit here and speak to you now. Also to thank the many, many people who have been with Caroline since that Easter Sunday way back in 1964. We are still here because you have given us such tremendous support. This is Radio Caroline it is now 12 midnight.*

After playing the 60s civil rights anthem, "We Shall Overcome" Johnnie Walker went on to say:-
Radio Caroline would like to extend its thanks to Mr. Harold Wilson and his Labour Government for at last, after over three and a half years of broadcasting, recognising this station's legality, its right to be here, its right to be broadcasting to Great Britain and the Continent, its right to give the music and service to the people of Europe which we have been doing since Easter Sunday 1964. We in turn recognise your right as our listener to have freedom of choice in your radio entertainment and of course that Radio Caroline belongs to you. It is your radio station even though it costs you nothing. And as we enter this new phase in our broadcasting history you naturally have our assurance that we intend to stay on the air, because we belong to you and we love you. Caroline continues!

The station's tender would now have to travel not from Essex, but from Holland, making a journey to and from the *Mi Amigo* of about 20 hours and any British staff would have to live abroad rather than run the risk of being arrested entering the UK. The Caroline North ship was to be tendered from Dundalk in the

Irish Republic, a journey of about 18 hours in good weather and the same restrictions applied to British staff on board the *Caroline* who were obliged, in theory at least, to take up residence abroad. In fact those who defiantly remained with the station did later return to Britain on a regular basis and, although the authorities were aware of this, no direct action was ever taken against them.

Radio Caroline North was, technically, not outlawed on 15th August as were all other offshore stations. This anomaly occurred because the station's ship was anchored off the coast of the Isle of Man - whose Government had refused to adopt the M.O.A. The Order in Council imposing the British version of the Act on the Island did not come into effect until 31st August, so supplies and personnel could quite legitimately be transferred to and from the ship using the Island's ports. However, most British staff on board the *Caroline* had

Caroline North's tender leaves Ramsey Harbour on its last supply run.

decided, like their southern colleagues to quit the station on 14th August for fear of prosecution.

On 31st August, at midnight Don Allen, Senior DJ on Caroline North, played the Manx National Anthem, thanked the Isle of Man Government and people for their continued support and announced:- *This is the Northern voice of Radio Caroline International on 259m, the continuing voice of free radio for the British Isles*. After a period of two weeks grace (and regular tender runs) because of a quirk in the legislative processes, Radio Caroline North and its crew had now officially joined its southern sister station in being totally isolated from Britain. Although they didn't know it at the time, it was to be another six weeks before a tender visited the radio ship again.

Following the implementation of the M.O.A. Radio Caroline became virtually cut off from Britain. Caroline House in London had been closed on 8th August and the station's operational headquarters transferred to an office in Amsterdam. Ronan O'Rahilly, as an Irish citizen, continued to operate quietly from an office at the former Radio Atlanta headquarters in Dean Street, London, using the cover of a company named Mid-Atlantic Films and in response to any enquiries from the press or authorities claimed to only be involved in the film production business. Although this was partially true the company also acted as a secret base for recruiting Radio Caroline staff and obtaining supplies of records.

Radio Caroline offices were also claimed to exist in New York, Paris and Toronto, but in fact the New York office was only an accommodation address in Madison Avenue and the Toronto office was the headquarters of Marich Associates - the company run by Terry Bate, who had been brought to the Caroline organisation in 1966 to help sell the station to prospective advertisers. Neither office in North America produced any real advertising contracts for Radio Caroline, although the number of American religious programmes aired by both the North and South stations did increase to about two hours a day during the latter part of 1967. Revenue from these sponsored religious programmes undoubtedly helped keep the stations on the air in the absence of any 'mainstream' advertising income.

The Paris office, too, did not succeed in generating advertising income for the station and plans to open further offices in Tokyo and Germany never came to fruition. The station's new address in Holland was not revealed to listeners for over two weeks, a factor which added further to the feeling of isolation for DJs on the radio ships who had been used to

receiving a regular supply of fan letters and record requests from their audiences.

What really did keep Radio Caroline on the air financially after 14th August was the heavy promotion of Major Minor records featuring artists such as David McWilliams, Raymond LeFevre and his Orchestra and the Roberto Mann Singers, as well as a large number of relatively unknown Irish folk singers. These 'plug' records -which numbered up to fourteen an hour at one point, were contained on a list supplied to both ships and DJs were instructed to play them to the exclusion of anything else they may have wished to include in their programmes.

Although financially necessary the directive from Philip Soloman (who was now effectively running the Caroline stations) to include these records in the station's output caused much resentment amongst DJs, particularly on Caroline South whose reception area contained hardly any audience for such material. Caroline North did at least have an audience in Ireland who appreciated the largely folk-based music, but saturation exposure of certain artists eventually became too much even for them.

A number of dummy 'announcements' and 'advertisements' from British companies were also broadcast at this time in an attempt to confuse the authorities, who were known to be monitoring the station's output. These dummy commercials also provided cover for any true advertisers who, it was claimed, had bought £300,000 worth of airtime - enough to keep the station operating for at least six months.

The fake advertisements which were broadcast included products from various large British companies such as Horlicks, Nestle and Beechams, who all strongly denied that they had bought airtime on the station in contravention of the new law. A spokesman for Beechams said, "All our contracts with the station ended last November. All they are doing is using old commercials and putting them out without our permission." Similar denials were issued by cigarette manufacturers Du Maurier, Peter Stuyvesant and Consulate as well as Swiss watch manufacturers Bulova, whose promotion continued to be aired at the top of each hour preceding the station's news bulletins.

Although much of what these companies claimed was true - and there was a lot of bluffing by Radio Caroline about its advertising income after 14th August 1967 - there were in fact still a number of contractural agreements with advertisers which the station happily continued to fulfil.

Vidor Batteries had signed a contract with Radio Caroline and Radio London for a three month campaign starting in June 1967, before the announcement of the implementation date of the M.O.A. and, therefore, although illegal by then both Caroline stations continued to promote its products until late 1967.

Another advertiser, Derek Gardner Photographics of Leatherhead and Epsom, had run a campaign on the station during the early summer of 1967 which included promotional offers available until the end of September. When Radio Caroline South continued to broadcast these commercials after 15th August, again in fulfillment of its contract, Derek Gardner visited the Amsterdam headquarters to deliver a personal protest to the station's management.

Another company, who had hardly ever advertised on offshore radio - Rowntrees Confectionery - also found many of its products, particularly Jelly Tots, Smarties, Spangles and Kit Kat being promoted on Radio Caroline after 15th August. In this instance the radio station had taped the soundtrack of television commercials and was re-broadcasting them as 'dummy' advertisements.

Officially Radio Caroline denied that they were transmitting any free advertisements and claimed that contracts for these international products had been entered into quite legally before the M.O.A. became effective.

Despite Radio Caroline's gesture of defiance in continuing to broadcast after 15th August the authorities in Britain were determined to enforce the legislation and prevent any further stations taking to the air.

The Post Office placed advertisements in over 70 newspapers and magazines warning potential advertisers and suppliers of the provisions of the M.O.A. and the penalties which could be imposed for contravening it. The publications carrying these advertisements included *The Times, Financial Times* and *Life* Magazine as well as local newspapers, particularly those circulating in areas which had been tendering bases for the offshore stations. A full page advertisement was also taken in the American magazine *Time*, in a bid to dissuade any foreign-based companies, particularly those in America, from buying airtime on Radio Caroline. Referring to the audiences left behind by the demise of the offshore stations the advertisements ended with the announcement that "The forthcoming BBC music programme will, the Government believes, meet the needs of these audiences."

Another more dramatic step taken by the authorities to prevent any more offshore stations coming on air was the demolition of the Sunk Head Tower, one of the wartime forts in the Thames Estuary. Unlike many of the other ex-Forts Sunk Head Tower, eleven miles off Felixstowe, was without doubt outside British territorial waters and therefore provided a safe potential base for a future radio or television station or supply facility. It had in fact been occupied by the unsuccessful Tower Radio project at the end of 1965 and early 1966, but had remained virtually abandoned since then because it was considered unstable.

On 18th August 1967 a team of twenty Royal Engineers landed on the Fort to begin cutting away the superstructure and lay explosive charges. Three days later 2,220 pounds of explosive were used to blow up the Tower, spreading debris across a half mile area of the Thames Estuary. The explosion itself could be clearly seen and heard by Radio Caroline South DJs on the *Mi Amigo,* who made a number of references to the Fort's demolition during their programmes that afternoon. When the smoke from the explosion had cleared all that remained of the Sunk Head Tower was the two concrete stumps which had once formed the legs of the Fort.

The initial euphoria which surrounded Radio Caroline's defiance of the new legislation soon subsided as practical operating difficulties came to the fore. By September 1967 both ships were (theoretically at least) being tendered from foreign ports - the *Mi Amigo* (Caroline South) from IJmuiden in Holland and the MV *Caroline* (Caroline North) from

Dundalk in Ireland. Fuel and major supplies for both ships came from Holland, but this involved a round trip which took over a week for the tender on a journey to the MV *Caroline* in Ramsey Bay. Both stations operated with just a few on-air staff and radio engineers, the two week on, one week off rotas had gone and DJs had to spend many weeks on board the ships without a break. Also, to provide airtime cover, programme shifts for the DJs were extended from the previous three hours to four, and sometimes even six hours at a time.

Programme material, and in particular new release records, also became more and more difficult to obtain and deliver to the ships, so quite quickly the station had to dispense with its Top 50 chart, although it tried to maintain the illusion of a chart for some weeks after 15th August.

Essential items of equipment and supplies were also in short supply and Caroline South in particular suffered from frequent transmitter breakdowns and periods off the air. Eventually, on 26th September, Radio Caroline South reduced its transmission hours from 24 hours a day to a 5.30am-2.00am schedule, the first tangible sign that the station was encountering severe difficulties in providing a full programme output and maintaining regular lines of supply.

Meanwhile, the much heralded replacement for the offshore stations, BBC Radio One was set to be launched on 30th September 1967. The station, which had been carved out of the BBC Light Programme (now itself re-named Radio Two) was to broadcast pop music from 7.00am-7.30pm each day and carry 'light entertainment' and easy listening music from 5.30am -7.00am and from 7.30pm until 2.00am the following morning.

The new station's Controller, Robin Scott, announced his DJ line up on 4th September which included fourteen from the offshore stations, the majority coming from Radio London. It was also revealed that the station would carry jingles, station identifications and promotions for other shows - based on the style and format of the offshore stations, but of course without any commercial announcements.

On 30th September the old Light Programme opened as usual at 5.30am and continued until just before 7.00am when former Caroline South and Radio London DJ Tony Blackburn launched the new BBC pop station.

Despite all the hype and promises that Radio One would be a replacement for the offshore stations it soon became apparent, even on that first day of broadcasting that it had retained much of the programming style of the old BBC Light Programme and it even simulcast many of the programmes which were intended primarily for Radio Two's older and less pop orientated audience.

Unfortunately on the day Radio One was launched Radio Caroline South, which should have provided listeners in the south of England with a real alternative, was experiencing severe technical problems and was either off the air for long periods or just playing continuous taped music.

Tenders visited the two Radio Caroline ships sporadically, often failing to bring essential items or sometimes even a replacement crew, a reflection of the difficulties of operating long distance supply routes. DJs spent many weeks at a time on board the two radio ships and the cumulative demoralising effect of this lifestyle came to be reflected in the station's programme output, dictated as it was largely by the Major Minor 'plug list'. Significantly neither those on board the ships, nor the station's listeners realised at this time that revenue earned from the constant playing of these 'plug list' records was not being used to pay Radio Caroline's bills.

However, despite this negative side to the continued operation of Radio Caroline some positive progress was achieved during the last two months of 1967. New DJs were clandestinely recruited to the station, including British as well as foreign passport holders and their arrival helped relieve some of the long on-air shifts and general feeling of isolation encountered by the original August 1967 'rebels' on both the Caroline ships.

Despite these clandestine recruitments and the facade of a foreign-based operation it had become common knowledge by late 1967 that Radio Caroline staff from both ships were quietly travelling in and out of Britain in contravention of the law, but without hindrance from the authorities. The Post

BBC Radio One's opening schedule, 30th September 1967

7.00am   **The Tony Blackburn Breakfast Show** -based on Radio London's format with jingles, promotions and Top 40 hits.

8.30am   **Junior Choice** - a new name for the old "Children's Favourites" programme dating back to the early 1950s.

9.55am   **Crack the Clue,** hosted by former Radio London DJ, Duncan Johnson A poor attempt to imitate the Caroline Cash Casino type of competition and without the big money prize!

10.00am   **Saturday Club** - a survivor from the Light Programme schedules this programme continued the use of BBC bands to play cover versions of hit records - essential to comply with the needle time restrictions imposed on the new station

12noon   **Midday Spin** hosted by former Caroline South DJ Emperor Rosko, the second (of only two) all record programmes in the Radio One schedule.

1.00pm   **The Jack Jackson Show** another legacy of the Light Programme, a mixture of big band music and comedy inserts.

1.55pm   **Crack the Clue** (repeat of the morning programme)

2.00pm   **Where It's At**, a magazine style programme, again from the old Light Programme, hosted by Chris Denning.

3.00pm   **Best of Newly Pressed**, another Light Programme show introduced by Pete Murray, playing new release records which were exempt from needle time restrictions.

4.00pm   **The Pete Brady Show**, an ex-Radio London DJ, but playing music from artists such as the Bert Weedon Quartet and Spencer's Washboard Kings, hardly Top 40 radio material.

5.30pm   **Country Meets Folk,** presented by Whally Whyton. As its name implies a specialist music programme, not for Top 40 radio.

6.30pm   **Scene and Heard** another topical pop magazine programme presented by Johnny Moran

7.30pm   Radio One then carried Radio Two's output until its closedown at 2.00am which included "Caterina Valente Sings", "Pete's People" introduced by Pete Murray with studio guests and live performances and "Night Ride" introduced by Sean Kelly and consisting largely of film soundtrack music, live guest performances and other non needle time music.

Office were fully aware of the operational difficulties being experienced by Radio Caroline, as well as its fragile financial situation, and seemed content to wait for the natural demise of the station rather than make folk heros out of individual DJs by prosecuting them for breaking the law.

As 1968 dawned both Radio Caroline stations were still on the air, each staffed by a small crew of DJs who had reluctantly become used to the hardships of an isolated life in the North Sea or Irish Sea. DJs frequently made on-air comments about the lack of supplies, equipment or records and morale generally fell to an all time low. Although they were still being paid regularly Radio Caroline's DJs were now earning roughly half the amount that 'star' DJs on Radio London or even Caroline itself were earning in late 1966 and early 1967.

In spite of the low morale one positive programming achievement at this time was the reintroduction of a US Hot 100 chart with a regular supply of records having been arranged from across the Atlantic. However on the financial side Ronan O'Rahilly admitted for the first time that Radio Caroline's income was below expectations and the prospect of actually making a profit from the station's operations seemed remote - a break-even on operating costs now appeared the only possibility.

RIDDLE OF RADIO CAROLINE SHIPS

Last of the pop pirates vanish

After struggling to overcome all sorts of practical difficulties and hardships to keep the Radio Caroline stations on the air for six months events took an unexpected and dramatic turn at the beginning of March 1968. During the afternoon of 2nd March a tug anchored a mile from the *Caroline* in Ramsey Bay, refusing to state its intended destination to the Isle of Man maritime authorities. The tug made no attempt to communicate either with the authorities or with the crew on board MV *Caroline*, who had themselves identified it as a Dutch vessel, but had no particular reason to suspect it was a threat to the radio ship.

Programming on both the North and South stations continued as normal that day with Radio Caroline North ending its transmissions shortly after 10.00pm following the regular Saturday night "Country and Western Jamboree", presented by Don Allen. Radio Caroline South closed at midnight following Johnnie Walker's programme, during which he had made a passing reference to the fact that the station may have to go off the air in the near future to enable the *Mi Amigo* to be dry docked for essential maintenance. The full irony of this remark, innocuous as it was at the time, became only too apparent the following morning.

In Ramsey Bay the DJs and crew of the *Caroline* were awoken at 2.00am on Sunday 3rd March by a loud thump as the tug *Utrecht* came alongside and Dutch seamen boarded the radio ship. They made for the Captain's cabin and summoned senior DJ Don Allen and the Chief Engineer to read a letter from the Wijsmuller Tender and Offshore Supply Co. stating that broadcasting was to cease, the studios were to be sealed and the transmitter crystal removed. Radio Caroline staff entered into a heated argument with the Dutch boarders about the legitimacy of their action, which amounted to piracy on the high seas, but with the threat of physical violence ever present they reluctantly complied with the instructions contained in the letter.

Meanwhile, staff on the *Mi Amigo*, unaware of what had happened to their sister ship during the night, opened transmissions of Radio Caroline South as usual at 5.00am on 3rd March with a half hour continuous music programme, prior to the start of Roger Day's Breakfast Show. However, that programme never began because at 5.20am the *Mi Amigo* was boarded by Dutch seamen from the tug *Titan* and the station was abruptly put off the air. An identical letter to that read to the Caroline North staff was then read to the Captain and crew of the *Mi Amigo* and, although the duty engineer tried to broadcast an emergency message the microphone was snatched from his hands and all broadcasting staff were locked in the ship's lounge.

The *Mi Amigo's* anchor was then raised by the Dutch crew and the silent radio ship was taken in tow by the *Titan.* In an obvious effort to confuse both those on board the *Mi Amigo* and outside observers the ship was first towed northwards to a position off East Anglia, where two more tugs joined the *Titan*. The tow then proceeded in an ever changing zig zag course across the North Sea with the ultimate destination uncertain at the time to all but the Dutch tug's crew.

In what had been a carefully planned and co-ordinated operation the tug *Utrecht* also attempted to take the *Caroline* in tow at 6.00am, but difficulties were experienced in raising the radio ship's anchor. In the end a decision was made to cut the anchor chain to release the *Caroline* and it was some twelve hours later before the tow actually commenced.

None of the staff on either radio ship knew for certain what was happening, other than the obvious fact that they had been forcibly put off the air. At first they didn't even know of their sister ship's fate. Those on board the *Mi Amigo* speculated that they were being towed to Holland for repairs, a scenario which had been hinted at by Johnnie Walker during his programme the previous evening. The *Mi Amigo* eventually arrived in Amsterdam on Monday 4th March and was docked "for normal repairs" according to a statement issued by the Wijsmuller company, which went on to say that, ultimately, the vessel would be returned to her anchorage and Radio Caroline could resume broadcasts.

The tow for the Caroline North ship, *Caroline*, was a much longer one lasting several days and she was shadowed for part of the journey by Royal Navy vessels. At first the crew thought the ship was heading for Greenore to be fitted with a new transmitter or, when it became obvious that this was not the case, they speculated that they may be going to take over Radio Caroline South broadcasts from off the Essex coast while the *Mi Amigo* was being repaired.

Neither theory proved to be correct and the *Caroline* arrived in Amsterdam on 8th March where she was docked near the *Mi Amigo*. The two radio ships were later moved to a shipyard and writs were attached to their masts, effectively detaining them in port. It became clear that Radio Caroline would not be returning to the air from either of these vessels in the near future.

After their arrival in Amsterdam staff were paid off, given tickets to fly back to Britain and told to await instructions to return - instructions which never came. Some DJs decided to wait in Holland for a while to see how the situation would develop hoping that somehow the ships would be released, while others returned home to Britain immediately.

The authorities did not stop or prosecute any of the Radio Caroline DJs when they re-entered Britain. The Post Office and the British Government had achieved what they wanted all along - the silencing of the last remaining offshore broadcaster, so it seemed unnecessarily petty to make scapegoats of individual DJs.

Although the Marine etc. Broadcasting (Offences) Act had been responsible for Radio Caroline's isolation it was not the provisions of the Act which finally brought about the station's demise. The real reason for the seizure of both ships lay in the financial management, or lack of it, within the Radio Caroline organisation itself. Wijsmullers had been contracted to provide a supply and servicing facility to both ships, but had not been paid since late 1967, although the money to do so was available from within the Caroline organisation. Wijsmuller's directors were divided amongst themselves over how to recover the money owed to them, some favoured negotiation with Radio Caroline's management while others, who won the day, preferred seizure of assets in lieu of the outstanding debts.

Philip Solomon, who by that time was the real force behind Radio Caroline, insisted that Wijsmuler put the ships back to sea before any debts would be paid, but the tender company insisted on payment first and continued to hold both ships in Amsterdam as security.

The Radio Caroline organisation put a brave face on the situation in early March 1968, promising that the station would return once repairs had been completed and insurance arrangements sorted out. However, with the continuing arguments over unpaid bills to the tender company there was no real chance of the station's immediate return from either the *Caroline* or the *Mi Amigo*, so Ronan O'Rahilly started to put together a package for re-launching the station from another vessel.

Together with a group of trusted ex-Caroline DJs (Don Allen, Jim Gordon, Roger Day, Andy Archer, Freddie Beare and Roger Scott) he devised a plan to try and relaunch the station from the former Radio 270 vessel *Oceaan VII*. This vessel was still up for sale in Whitby Harbour and O'Rahilly, using the psuedonym O'Connor, made a number of visits to the Yorkshire port to negotiate the purchase of the ship through the local estate agents. He planned to anchor *Oceaan VII* off Frinton-on-Sea, Essex and resume broadcasts of Radio Caroline on Easter Sunday 1968.

However, press reporters obtained information about this plan and published the story of Radio Caroline's Easter return. Although at the time this advance publicity was blamed for the failure of the scheme, negotiations for the purchase of the *Oceaan VII* had in fact already fallen through. The only other ex-offshore radio ship still available, the *Galaxy*, (former home of Radio London, now docked in

Hamburg), was briefly considered by Ronan O'Rahilly but the price being asked for this vessel was thought to be too high.

With the last British offshore station of the 1960's now silent many listeners started tuning to the broadcasts of Radio Veronica which was still transmitting from off the Dutch coast. This station, which had witnessed the arrival and demise of British offshore radio, started to receive an enormous amount of mail from British listeners who preferred tuning to a foreign language broadcast they could hardly understand, rather than BBC Radio One the 'replacement' for their own offshore stations.

In response to this increase in its English speaking audience Radio Veronica introduced some English programming in June 1968 and even engaged former Radio Caroline South DJ Robbie Dale, to present a show four evenings a week. This was some, albeit small, consolation for a generation of English speaking offshore radio listeners, who reluctantly now had to face the fact that perhaps the Government had won after all and there would be no more offshore stations anchored off the British coast.

Vox Pop

The day Radio Caroline closed was miserable, not just because of the weather, but nobody knew for certain what had happened.

At first we hoped it was just a technical failure and music would burst out of the radio again at any moment.

But nothing happened all day - I think it was a Sunday - then in the evening we saw on the television news that the ship had been towed away. We knew then that something serious was wrong.

I refused to tune to the BBC as a principle - we had all fought for 'free radio' after all and Radio One wasn't what we wanted to listen to.

Graham (Braintree, Essex)

Chapter 10   ... and the beat goes on

Although by March 1968 all the British offshore radio stations had closed, that was not the end of the story – far from it.

In 1970 two Swiss businessmen, who had been involved in an earlier plan to start an offshore radio station off the German coast using the former Radio London ship, *Galaxy*,

Tune in & TURN ON

RNi

Radio NorthSea International 220 m.

launched Radio Northsea International (RNI), at first as a dual language English and German station, then as an English only service and later as a Dutch and English language station.

RNI operated from the ship *Mebo II*, initially anchored off the Dutch coast, then off the Essex coast from where it was jammed by the Labour government during the run-up to the June 1970 General Election.

For a week immediately preceding the General Election the station changed its name to Radio Caroline and Free Radio groups mounted a huge campaign, particularly in the marginal constituencies in the south-east of England, urging listeners to vote for Conservative candidates.

During the week (despite the jamming signal which was produced from a powerful transmitter at a Royal Navy base) announcements were regularly made over the station promoting the arguments in favour of commercial radio and asking listeners to vote Conservative. As well as the on-air promotions a campaign bus toured London and south-east marginal constituencies to publicise Radio Caroline and the 'fight for free radio'.

The Conservatives unexpectedly won the General Election and, although there is no conclusive proof of the effect of Radio

Caroline's campaign, a large number of south-east marginal constituencies were taken by Conservative candidates, which helped the party gain a majority in parliament. Despite optimistic hopes for support from the new government, the jamming did not stop, nor did the introduction of commercial radio into the UK rise very high on the political agenda.

After the General Election the station changed its name back to RNI and the *Mebo II* sailed back to the Dutch coast to avoid the continued jamming. However, three months later, in September, RNI closed – it had been paid to do so by the hugely popular Dutch offshore station, Radio Veronica, who feared a rival off the coast of Holland would, in the short term attract advertising revenue from them and, in the longer term, would jeopardise their chances of obtaining a land-based licence.

By the end of 1970 the owners of RNI had decided to reopen their station. After offering to pay back the money to Radio Veronica – and having it refused – the *Mebo II* was 'repossessed' and in January 1971 RNI returned to the airwaves, broadcasting an English language service and later a Dutch daytime service.

RNI broadcast on medium wave, short wave and FM and reception was possible, although not perfect, across a large area of Britain and Europe. In the absence of any alternative (Radio One programming had still not fully replaced the 60's offshore stations as far as many listeners were concerned and the first local commercial stations were still over two years away) RNI proved hugely popular, but the English language service attracted relatively little advertising.

Another offshore station made a brief appearance off the Dutch coast in the summer of 1970 – Capital Radio – broadcasting from the *King David*. Unfortunately because of continuous problems with the ship's unique ring aerial (as opposed to a vertical aerial mast) the station never really became established and closed after is ship ran aground during a storm in November 1970.

Although Radio Caroline was off the air, Ronan O'Rahilly and others were still looking for ways of bringing the station back. There was a brief period in 1969/70 when plans were announced for Caroline TV, to be broadcast from a Constellation aircraft flying over the North Sea, but although a number of start dates were given, nothing ever happened and the project quietly faded from public attention.

However, by the summer of 1972 the Wijsmuller Company had decided to dispose of the two Caroline ships which had been rusting away in Amsterdam for over four years. The MV *Caroline* was sold for scrap and the *Mi Amigo* was purchased by Dutch free radio supporter, Gerard van Dam, who announced plans for the ship to be turned into a radio museum. During the course of this 'conversion' Ronan O'Rahilly persuaded Gerard van Dam to use the ship to re-launch Radio Caroline and at the end of September 1972 test broadcasts started again from the *Mi Amigo*, now anchored off the Dutch coast within sight of Radio Veronica and RNI.

These were turbulent times and Radio Caroline had many problems- technical and organisational - including failing equipment, mast collapses, supply and staffing difficulties and a mutiny amongst the Dutch crew which resulted in the ship being taken into port and having to be clandestinely 'released' at the end of December 1972.

Throughout the early part of 1973 Radio Caroline was frequently off the air with continuing technical problems. By April the generator equipment had failed completely and the *Mi Amigo* was once again silent.

However misfortune for another offshore station provided an opportunity for Caroline. In mid April, Radio Veronica's ship *Norderney* ran aground during a storm and Radio Caroline offered the *Mi Amigo* as a temporary home for the Dutch station, which agreed to pay for replacement equipment to be installed.

Radio Veronica programmes were broadcast from the *Mi Amigo* for ten days and the income this brought enabled the Caroline organisation to replace some equipment and install a new aerial mast. By June 1973 Radio Caroline was back in business broadcasting pop music on two frequencies – one English language and one Dutch - with an overnight English service of 'progressive' music.

In mid July 1973 a new Flemish language station, Radio Atlantis, hired airtime from the Caroline organisation and broadcast to audiences in Belgium and Holland for 13 hours a day. After Radio Atlantis had closed for the day Caroline launched an English language 'progressive' music station – Radio Seagull – which broadcast overnight, but the music played was often very obscure and failed to attract large audiences. The station also promoted love, peace and happiness – a throwback to the 60's hippie era, but a concept which was later to re-emerge on Radio Caroline under the title 'Loving Awareness'.

By the beginning of October the *Mi Amigo* was once again experiencing technical difficulties when the newly constructed aerial mast collapsed. At about this time too, Radio Atlantis acquired its own ship, the *Jeanine*, and its broadcasts were transferred to the new vessel.

Not all was lost however, another Belgian businessman, Sylvan Tack, wanted to launch his own offshore station and struck a deal with Ronan O'Rahilly to hire airtime using the call sign Radio Mi Amigo. Another new aerial mast was constructed on the *Mi Amigo*, but the work was hampered by North Sea storms and took months longer than anticipated to complete. Eventually Radio Mi Amigo was launched on New Year's Day 1974 and became an extremely successful station, serving Belgium and Holland, but also attracting a sizeable audience in southern England.

Radio Seagull also made a brief return at the beginning of 1974, broadcasting at night after Radio

Mi Amigo's programmes had finished. Then in February Radio Caroline was re-launched with a format similar to Radio Seagull, but based on album tracks rather than singles.

So, by the early months of 1974 listeners in southern England could tune into five offshore radio stations – RNI, Radio Mi Amigo, Radio Caroline, Radio Atlantis and Radio Veronica – and although much of the programming for these stations was directed at Dutch and Belgian audiences many in Britain preferred their output to the BBC or the fledgling Independent Local Radio network which had a few stations scattered across the country.

Just as the second offshore radio boom was at its height the Dutch Government introduced its version of the Marine Offences Act. The legislation came into effect on 1st September 1974 and led to the closure of three of the offshore stations - RNI, Radio Atlantis and the long established Radio Veronica. However, as in 1967, Radio Caroline (and Radio Mi Amigo) stood alone, defied the new law and continued to broadcast, but the *Mi Amigo* sailed to a new anchorage off the British coast, with tendering and supplies ostensibly carried out from Spain.

Radio Caroline and Radio Mi Amigo continued broadcasting from the *Mi Amigo* anchored off the British coast for a few more years and during that time experienced numerous problems with equipment, the

weather and tendering and supply arrangements. A number of people were prosecuted in Britain and Europe for their involvement with the continued operation of the offshore stations and even an episode where the radio ship drifted inside British territorial waters and was raided by the police did little to prevent broadcasts continuing on a fairly regular, if at times, intermittent basis.

In October 1978 Radio Mi Amigo left the Caroline ship, which at the time was again

suffering from technical failures and a shortage of diesel fuel. However six months later Radio Caroline returned to the airwaves with a new Dutch language service in addition to the English service. The Dutch service proved very popular with listeners and advertisers and further income was generated from numerous sponsored American religious programmes, broadcast on the English service.

A couple of other smaller offshore radio stations also came on the air for short periods during 1978 and 1979 – Radio Delmare from off the Dutch coast and Radio Mi Amigo (now known as Mi Amigo 272) made a brief return from another ship, the *Magdalena*, in 1979.

Both the Dutch and English services of Radio Caroline continued virtually as scheduled throughout the first three months of 1980, but disaster was just around the corner. Gales and heavy seas returned to the North Sea on 19th March, but listeners remained virtually unaware of the drama unfolding on the *Mi Amigo* because the taped Dutch Service programmes continued to be broadcast as normal.

The only hint of a problem came in a series of coded messages broadcast in English at the top of each hour. The numbers were, of course meaningless to the majority of listeners, but for those involved with the operation of the station they indicated that something was seriously wrong on board the radio ship. By the time the English Service was due to start at 7pm, listeners became more aware that something was wrong because the station just played continuous music, with the hourly coded announcements.

The *Mi Amigo* had drifted during the day, hit a sandbank and without warning started to take in a large amount of water – too much for the pumps to cope with. The four staff on board were rescued (along with the ship's canary!) in an extremely dangerous operation carried out by the Sheerness lifeboat. Before the rescued crew had reached shore the *Mi Amigo*, home to so many radio stations for more than 18 years, had sunk leaving her aerial mast standing above the waterline. The mast survived in that position for a further six years before itself collapsing beneath the waves.

Almost as soon as the *Mi Amigo* had sunk rumours began to circulate about the return of

Radio Caroline, and these were to continue for a number of years, with many false starts being announced. Behind the scenes plans were being made, but as with all offshore radio projects these had to be undertaken in great secrecy for fear of arousing official 'interest'. A new ship, the *Ross Revenge*, was acquired in 1981, but it was to be a further two years before Radio Caroline was heard on the airwaves again, thanks to legal wrangles with the North American backers and problems over the ownership of the new ship.

At the beginning of August 1983 the *Ross Revenge* sailed from Spain where she had been fitted out as a broadcasting vessel, including the construction of a 300' aerial mast, and anchored off the British coast, near where the *Mi Amigo* had sunk three years earlier.

Radio Caroline returned to the air on 20th August 1983 with an album-based format directed towards an adult audience in the 18-40 age group -the new Radio Caroline did not intend to compete with the growing number of Top 40 stations which were coming on the air in Britain. Nevertheless listeners were pleased to have Radio Caroline back whatever its format and, although radically different from the station that had broadcast in the 1960's, the concept of freedom and the right to free speech that Caroline stood for struck a chord with very many people. In addition a new generation of listeners who had been too young to remember the 1960's offshore radio boom were now tuning in to Radio Caroline, and found the station's output a welcome alternative to what was available elsewhere.

LIVE FROM THE NORTH SEA ON **319** Metres (963khz)
Europe's first and only album station
RADIO CAROLINE
FOR THE BEST IN MUSIC; THE TIME OF YOUR LIFE

The new format did not please everyone, however, and came in for some sharp criticism from the weekly music paper *Melody Maker* at the end of December:-

The music largely played on the station is now unexpectedly conservative – a safe, predictable mixture of AOR Rock and old classics, with a smattering of soul and selected current chart material between. Caroline rarely play anything on an independent label and the only thing even vaguely revolutionary about their format is how little emphasis they put on the jocks themselves.

Caroline's new format was also about to be challenged by yet another offshore radio station. The all-American Top 50 format station, Laser, broadcasting from the MV *Communicator* - anchored within sight of the *Ross Revenge* - started test broadcasts in January 1984, but experienced technical problems with a new aerial, supposedly held aloft by a helium balloon. Laser 558 did eventually launch with a more conventional aerial arrangement installed on the ship in May 1984 and became an immediate success with listeners in Britain and northern Europe.

LASER558
all europe radio

The slick presentation style and 'more music, less talk' policy of Laser 558 appealed to listeners who were dissatisfied with the stale BBC Radio One and Independent Local Radio stations, but who still wanted to hear Top 40 music. Similarly the station also appealed to older listeners who could remember the heyday of 1960's offshore stations such as Radio London and Radio England.

Caroline was forced to consider reacting to its new neighbour - not only was Laser's format having more appeal with audiences but its frequency (558kHz) was penetrating further into the south east of England than Caroline's signal on 963kHz. Caroline experimented with a number of alternative frequencies and finally started simultaneous broadcasts on two frequencies throughout the autumn of 1984.

The real reason for these tests was revealed in December 1984 when a new Dutch language offshore station – Radio Monique – came on the air from the *Ross Revenge*. Once again the Caroline organisation had hired its facilities to a revenue-earning foreign language broadcaster, an essential move in the absence of any real advertising income on the English station.

While Monique and Caroline continued to broadcast to their respective audiences, Laser 558 was experiencing increasing technical and revenue problems as well as attracting unwelcome attention from the authorities, prompted by a number of ILR stations in the south east, which felt they were losing audiences to the offshore rival.

This increased attention culminated in a surveillance operation, mounted by the Department of Trade and Industry, throughout the summer months of 1985. In what became nicknamed 'Euroseige 85' an ocean-going launch was hired by the British authorities to keep a watch on the two radio ships and the various clandestine tendering vessels which serviced them. This expensive operation, reportedly costing taxpayers over £100,000 continued throughout the summer and autumn of 1985 and seriously hampered tendering arrangements for both radio ships.

A major power failure on board the *Communicator* in November 1985 put an end to Laser 558 and forced the radio ship to sail into Harwich, where she was impounded by the British authorities. With the *Communicator* in port the surveillance operation was called off, leaving the *Ross Revenge*, and the two stations on board, to continue broadcasting without further undue hindrance.

With Laser 558 off the air Radio Caroline quickly changed its frequency and format to try and attract Laser's audience. Caroline broadcast for 24 hours a day on 558kHz and there was a move away from the totally album based format with Top 40 and 60's and 70's classics being introduced. At the beginning of 1986 Radio Caroline introduced two separate services throughout the night. On the

frequency used during the day by Radio Monique 'Caroline Overdrive' was launched with the familiar rock and album music format, while the 558 service continued with its pop and classics format. These format changes led to Radio Caroline increasing in popularity and a audience survey in 1986 showed the station outperforming all the ILR stations in East Anglia while in the general south east area it was more popular than London's Capital Radio.

Despite these optimistic initiatives and achievements practical difficulties continued to dominate the station's life – supply difficulties, haphazard tendering, bad weather and a broken anchor chain which resulted in the *Ross Revenge* going adrift all eventually led to a reduction in the 24 hour output. By February 1986 the station was closing at 1.00am and a shortage of DJs meant that those on board were presenting double programme shifts, while at other times just continuous music was being played. Radio Caroline's only real income source at this time was from sponsored American religious programmes and they were consolidated into a separate service – Viewpoint 963.

Meanwhile the former Laser 558 ship, *Communicator*, had been repaired and sold and was eventually granted a seaworthiness certificate, enabling her to leave port in November 1986. At the beginning of December a new station – Laser Hot Hits – was launched, much to the embarrassment of the British authorities, who twelve months previously thought they had silenced the station for good.

Success for Laser Hot Hits was short-lived, however, as numerous technical problems forced the station off the air for days, sometimes weeks. The station eventually closed at Easter, although the *Communicator* remained at sea and even moved (along with the *Ross Revenge*) when the government introduced a new twelve mile territorial waters limit in October 1987. Much work was carried out on board the ship during the silent months of that summer, but a plans to launch two new stations – Starforce and Harmony – came to nothing due to financial problems, although there was an attempt to make some test broadcasts at the end of October 1987.

During the night of 15/16th October 1987 a hurricane swept across south east England, causing major destruction and loss of power supplies throughout a huge area. At sea the silent *Communicator* dragged her anchor and drifted some 25 miles, while the *Ross Revenge* held her anchor, but the huge aerial mast took a buffeting from the storm. When calm weather returned everyone on board was relieved to see that the 300' mast was still standing and Radio Caroline and Radio Monique were able to continue broadcasting virtually as normal.

Towards the end of November another storm hit the North Sea, increasing in intensity as the day went on and whipping up heavy seas which caused the *Ross Revenge* to pitch and roll. During the early hours of 25th November 1987 the radio ship's aerial tower, weakened by the buffeting from the October hurricane, collapsed over the starboard side, putting both stations off the air. Although no one knew for certain at the time, Radio Monique was never to return from its offshore base, but those behind Radio Caroline were more determined.

The Caroline organisation desperately needed to find a way of putting the radio ship back on the air and earning revenue, particularly from the sponsored American religious programmes on the Viewpoint service. Incredibly an emergency replacement aerial system was installed at sea in appalling weather conditions and Radio Caroline returned with a very low power service at the beginning of December.

By the beginning of 1988 various attempts were being made to improve the emergency aerial system on the *Ross Revenge*. After a number of failed attempts a new lattice work mast was acquired and transported to the radio ship in a series of clandestine tendering trips from small British harbours. The new mast was in place by the summer of 1988 and in July a new Dutch language service – Radio 558 (later changed to Radio 819) began broadcasting during daytime hours. Radio Caroline initially maintained its own English language overnight service, but with an extension constructed on the aerial mast, enabling the Dutch station to move frequencies Caroline introduced a full daytime

service on 558kHz from November. A short-wave service, World Mission Radio, was also started from the *Ross Revenge* to broadcast various sponsored American religious programmes.

Despite all the ups and downs experienced by those operating Radio Caroline over the years the station was on the air and able to celebrate its Silver Jubilee in 1989 with a major broadcast of the all time Top 1001 records over the Easter weekend. Radio Caroline's 25th anniversary was also featured in the national press and television as well as a

Pop pirates silenced

CAROLINE IS SCUPPERED

Caroline knocked off the airwaves

Dutch police raid pirate radio ship

DJs slug it out as Dutch shut Radio Caroline

number of tribute programmes broadcast by local radio stations.

The euphoria of achieving 25 years broadcasting was short-lived. By mid-summer 1989 there was increased surveillance activity taking place around the *Ross Revenge*, hampering fuel supplies and causing staffing and programming difficulties. On land, the Dutch authorities were conducting a number of raids on premises thought to be associated with one or more of the radio stations broadcasting from the *Ross Revenge*. Then on 19th August Dutch and British officials mounted a boarding operation on the *Ross Revenge*, anchored in international waters. The raiders stripped out broadcasting equipment, emptied the record library and tried to persuade all those on board to leave the radio ship. Although some Dutch staff from Radio 819 did agree to leave the British nationals on board decided to stay with the, now silent, *Ross Revenge*.

In the six weeks following the raid Radio Caroline's engineer, Peter Chicago, almost single-handedly managed to re-build a medium wave transmitter from spare parts which had been hidden from the raiding party and from the wreckage of what was left of the shortwave transmitter. As a result of this achievement Radio Caroline was able to start broadcasting again at the beginning of October, with two DJs who had remained on board since the raid, Dave Asher and Caroline Martin sharing the programme hours until gradually more personnel were able to re-join the *Ross Revenge*. Yet again Radio Caroline had managed to defiantly provide a service for its listeners, despite all the efforts by the authorities to silence the station for good.

Radio Caroline struggled along throughout the first six months of 1990, despite enormous difficulties with supplying the *Ross Revenge* and declining morale amongst the staff on board the radio ship. The station was off the air for much of the late summer, although a

special broadcast was made on 19th August to commemorate the first anniversary of the raid on the *Ross Revenge*. After that programming became more and more sporadic and during September and October 1990 various transmissions were broadcast when fuel supplies were available and the increasingly malfunctioning equipment allowed.

What was to be Caroline's final broadcast from international waters took place on the evening of 4th/5th November 1990. After that the transmitter was switched off because fuel was in such short supply that literally every drop had to be used to keep the generator running just to provide lighting on board the ship.

On land too events were conspiring against Radio Caroline. The new London ILR station, Spectrum Radio, was allocated the same frequency as used by Radio Caroline – 558kHz and these broadcasts inevitably interfered with the offshore station's weak signal. New legislation was also on the horizon in the form of the Broadcasting Bill, which included sweeping powers for British authorities to enlist military support to board and silence foreign registered offshore radio ships, even though they were anchored outside territorial limits in international waters. The Bill's provisions also gave immunity to those

involved in any such raid, so there was no possibility of legal action being taken by station owners to recover their ship or equipment if it were seized.

The British Department of Trade and Industry made it clear that they fully intended to use their new powers under the Broadcasting Act to forcibly board the ship using military personnel and a Radio Caroline spokesman claimed that they even had knowledge of a date for the proposed raid – 5th January 1991. The Radio Caroline organisation had no choice but to keep the radio ship silent while they tried to find a legal way of returning to the air.

One possibility was to obtain a licence from another country to broadcast programmes, effectively making the radio ship and station part of that country's broadcasting system. This apparent loophole in the new legislation proved more theoretical than practical however and despite claims of negotiations with the Liberian government nothing ever came of the proposal.

Although the *Ross Revenge* was silent Radio Caroline experimented with other outlets during 1991– shortwave broadcasts from a US based station and the then newly emerging facility of satellite radio. Neither was very successful and could not claim to attract large audiences, but nevertheless Radio Caroline still had a presence on the air, even if it was only for a few hours a week.

A skeleton crew remained at sea with the *Ross Revenge* throughout 1991, but on 19th November during a severe storm the radio ship broke from her anchor chain and drifted onto the notorious Goodwin Sands, graveyard to hundreds of ships over the years. An RAF helicopter mounted a rescue operation, taking the six crew members off the stricken radio ship, which was reported to be in danger of capsizing.

Against all the odds the *Ross Revenge* managed to stay upright throughout the storm and a Dover Harbour Board tug later managed to land a salvage crew on the vessel and tow her from the sandbank – one of only a handful of vessels ever to be rescued from the Goodwin Sands. The radio ship was towed to Dover Harbour and impounded as unseaworthy.

The story of Radio Caroline at sea had ended. The station's owners and the *Ross Revenge* Supporters Group negotiated and eventually succeeded in paying off the salvage costs and the *Ross Revenge* has been extensively repaired and renovated. The vessel has had a number of temporary anchorages since her rescue from the Goodwin Sands, but always close to the shore – for years the Detention Order was only relaxed, not removed, because she was still not considered fully seaworthy despite years of renovation work by volunteer supporters.

The ship has been used as a broadcasting base again, including venues off Clacton, in London Docklands and at Southend Pier, but this time for officially licensed, month long, low power broadcasts under the Restricted Service Licence system operated by the former Radio Authority. Radio Caroline as a radio station has managed to stay on the air, primarily on satellite services and its broadcasts are currently available on Sky digital and on the internet, as well as via the Worldspace satellite radio network.

The *Ross Revenge* anchored off Clacton in August 1995, during a month long Restricted Service Licence broadcast

The equipment and record collection removed in the 1989 raid has now been returned by the Dutch authorities and much of it has been re-installed on the *Ross Revenge*, which is currently moored in Rochester, Kent, where volunteer supporters continue to lovingly repair and maintain the radio ship as a tangible legacy of Radio Caroline's forty years of broadcasting and an era of radio history, the like of which will never be seen again.

Appendix 1 The Ships

Caroline

Former Name(s)	*Fredericia*
Description	Danish passenger ferry
Length/Tonnage	200'/693tons
Built	1930
Flag State	Panama
Stations Housed	Radio Caroline, Caroline North
Ultimate Fate	Scrapped 1980

Cheeta 2

Former Name(s)	*Habat*
Description	Passenger ship
Length/Tonnage	/450tons
Built	1924
Flag State	Panama/Honduras
Stations Housed	Radio Mercur, Skanes Radio Mercur, Radio Syd, TV Syd, Caroline South
Ultimate Fate	Sailed to Gambia in 1967, Used as a floating restaurant, sank in Gambia River 1971.

Comet

Former Name(s)	——
Description	Irish lightship
Length/Tonnage	90'/500 tons
Built	1904
Flag State	Panama
Stations Housed	Radio Scotland; Radio Scotland and Ireland, Radio 242
Ultimate Fate	Towed to Holland and used as a houseboat.

Galaxy

Former Name(s)	*Admirable; Density*
Description	US Navy minesweeper, cargo vessel
Length/Tonnage	185'/780 tons
Built	1944
Flag State	Panama; Honduras
Stations Housed	Radio London
Ultimate Fate	Lay derelict for many years in Germany. Sank at quayside in Keil, 1979. Scrapped 1986

Laissez Faire

Former Name(s)	*FS263, Deal; Don Carlos; Olga Patricia*
Description	Military landing craft; general cargo ship
Length/Tonnage	117'/562 tons
Built	1944
Flag State	Panama
Stations Housed	Radio England; Britain Radio; Radio Dolfijn; Radio 355; Radio 227
Ultimate Fate	Re-named *Akuarius II* (1970). *Earl J Conrad Jnr.* (1974). Used as fishing vessel in the Gulf of Mexico.

Mi Amigo

Former Name(s)	*Margarethe; Olga; Bon Jour; Magda Maria*
Description	As *Margarethe* -three masted schooner; as *Olga* cargo vessel
Length/Tonnage	98' (as *Margarethe*) 134' (as *Olga*) /470tons
Built	1921, lengthened 1927
Flag State	Nicaragua (for Radio Nord) Panama (for Radio Atlanta and Radio Caroline)
Stations Housed	Radio Nord; Radio Atlanta; Radio Caroline South; Radio 199; Radio Caroline; Radio Veronica; Radio Atlantis; Radio Seagull; Radio Mi Amigo
Ultimate Fate	Sank 20th March 1980. Later destroyed as a hazard to shipping.

Oceaan VII

Former Name(s)	*Scheveningen 330*
Description	Lugger
Length/Tonnage	118'/179 tons
Built	1939
Flag State	Honduras
Stations Housed	Radio 270
Ultimate Fate	Scrapped 1968

Appendix 2 The Sea Forts

In 1941 the Admiralty and the War Office decided that more anti-aircraft protection was needed for London and Merseyside. Amphibious forts were proposed as a solution and two distinctive designs were prepared by G A Maunsell, a prominent civil engineer engaged by the Government. Maunsell's designs were for four forts to be used by the Navy in the waters of the North Sea off the Essex coast and six forts for use by the Army, three in the Thames Estuary and three in Liverpool Bay.

NAVY FORTS

The Navy forts comprised a boat shaped reinforced concrete pontoon which carried two round towers topped by a steel deck housing armament and radar equipment. There was some initial concern in the Admiralty that the structures may become unstable due to the clay and soft shingle on the seabed of the Thames Estuary. To check this a study was made of ships which had sunk in that area and it was found that where vessels had sunk end-on to the tideway they had hardly been affected by scouring or subsidence. Accordingly the sea forts were similarly positioned so that their pontoons were lying with the tidal current.

The forts were largely prefabricated and were constructed and assembled in a specially converted dry dock basin at Gravesend by Holloway Brothers Ltd. The two towers of the forts each contained seven decks housing fuel, ammunition, water, generators and crew accommodation. The main deck had officers accommodation, while the Bofors Deck had fresh and sea water tanks as well as ventilation equipment and the main gun defences. The Control Room was fitted with telephones, radio and early radar equipment linked by landline to a shore-based HQ. At the front of each tower was a lattice steel mooring platform, known as a Dolphin, fitted with a crane used for loading supplies.

When each fort had been commissioned and equipped it was towed by tugs to its grounding position with a full compliment of crew aboard. When the forts were in position the hollow pontoons were gradually flooded with seawater until they sank to the seabed, in an operation taking less than half an hour. The first tow (Roughs Tower) started in January 1942 but due to bad weather had to be postponed until early February.

During the grounding of Tongue Sands Fort enemy aircraft were spotted approaching, the fort had to be crash dived, going into action immediately. This crash diving resulted in the fort having a slight list and it proved to be less stable than the other forts. For this reason it was considered unsuitable for use as a broadcasting base by the 60s offshore stations.

The four Navy forts were credited with shooting down 22 enemy aircraft, sinking one E boat, badly damaging another and destroying 20-30 V1 flying bombs. There were also numerous rescue missions mounted from the forts for pilots who had been forced to ditch in the North Sea.

The four Navy forts and their involvement in offshore radio were:-

Roughs Tower Never used for broadcasting purposes, but was the subject of fierce battles between rival offshore radio groups because it was the only one outside British territorial limits. It was finally taken over by Roy Bates and declared an independent Principality - Sealand - in 1967. Various plans were announced to develop and extend the Fort for leisure purposes but these came to nothing. The Territorial Sea Act 1987 finally brought Roughs Tower inside British territorial limits.

Sunk Head Used briefly by Radio Tower/Tower Radio this fort was demolished by Royal Marines in August 1967 to prevent its further use by any offshore radio station either as a broadcasting or supply base.

Knock John Used by Radio Essex and BBMS, but abandoned in favour of Roughs Tower by Roy Bates after a court ruling in 1966 that the fort was inside British territorial waters.

Tongue Sands The least stable of the Navy forts it was not used by any offshore broadcaster, although it was briefly considered by Roy Bates as a possible base for his planned second station, Radio Kent/Radio Albatross. The fort finally collapsed into the sea during a Force 11 gale on 22nd February 1996.

ARMY FORTS

The Army forts were designed to conform as far as possible to the format of a shore based battery, with emphasis on anti-aircraft defence. Each fort, which consisted of seven separate towers linked by catwalks, had four heavy and two light guns with a central Control Room and a searchlight position. The Thames Estuary forts were also built by Holloway Brothers Ltd. at Gravesend while the Mersey Forts were built at Bromborough Docks.

The fort complex as a whole comprised a central control tower surrounded by five further gun towers and a searchlight tower to the rear. Each individual tower had a base of reinforced concrete supporting four pre-cast hollow concrete legs, braced by a steel frame. The superstructure on top of the legs consisted of an octagonal building with 6mm thick steel plated walls, containing three decks. Each tower carried its own supply of fresh and seawater, while the Bofors Gun tower and the searchlight tower carried fuel supplies. All fuel and water supply tanks were linked by a network of pipes along the interconnecting catwalks.

When built each tower was towed to its grounding position between two specially constructed barges and positioned on the sea-bed by pumping compressed air into the hollow legs. The first tower to be put in position was always the central Bofors Gun tower which could then protect the others as they were lowered The whole operation, including the installation of the inter-connecting catwalks took several days to complete.

The three Thames Estuary Army forts and their involvement with offshore radio were:-

Great Nore (code name U5). This was demolished in 1959 as it was considered too much of a hazard in the main shipping lanes following a collision involving a Swedish ship.

Red Sands (code name U6). Used by Radio Invicta, KING Radio and Radio 390. This was the only one of the Thames Estuary Army forts to remain intact.

Shivering Sands (code name U7). Used by Radio Sutch and Radio City. One of the towers was demolished as the result of a ship colliding with it in the early 1950's, killing four men.

The Army forts in the Mersey Estuary were all demolished in the early 1950s as they were considered to be a danger to shipping.

Bibliography

There have been a number of other books published covering the subject of offshore broadcasting, although many are no longer in print.

The following cover British offshore radio and in some cases other offshore stations around the world:-

Who's Who in Pop Radio, Peter Alex, New Englsih Library, 1966

Radio Caroline, John Venmore Rowland, Landmark Press, 1967

When Pirates Ruled the Waves, Paul Harris, Impulse Publications, 1968

Offshore Radio, Gerry Bishop, Iceni Enterprises, 1975

Broadcasting from the High Seas, Paul Harris, Paul Harris Publishing, 1977

Butterfly Upon the Wheel, Peter Moore, Offshore Echo's Magazine, 1982

The Lid off Laser, Paul Rusling, Pirate Publications, 1984

SOS – 10 Days in the Life of a Lady, Simon Barrett, Paul Harris Publishing, 1984

Last of the Pirates, Bob Noakes, Paul Harris Publishing, 1985 (ISBN 0 86228 0923)

Selling the Sixties, Robert Chapman, Routledge 1992 (ISBN 0 415 07970 5)

Pop Went the Pirates, Keith Skues, Lambs Meadow Publications, 1994 (ISBN 0 907398 03 0)

From International Waters – 60 Years of Offshore Broadcasting, Mike Leonard, Forest Press 1996 (ISBN 0 9527684 0 2)

The Wonderful Radio London Story, Chris Elliot, East Anglian Productions, 1997 (ISBN 1 901854 00)

Radio 270, Life on the Oceaan Waves, Bob Preedy, 2002 (ISBN 1 8743660 2 0)

Radio Caroline – the Pirate Years, Ralph C Humphries, Oakwood Press, 2003 (ISBN 0 85361 611 6)

The Ship that Rocked the World, Tom Lodge, The Umi Foundation, 2003 (ISBN 0 9695938 5 6)

In addition these books (in English) have been published about some of the foreign offshore radio stations:-

History of Radio Nord, Jack Kotschack, Forlags AB, Stockholm, 1963 and Impulse Publications 1970

De Veronica Sage, Gareth van Zanten, Teleboek NV 1968 (A history of the Dutch radio station, Radio Veronica)

The Shoestring Pirates, Adrian Blackburn, Hodder and Stoughton (New Zealand) 1974 (ISBN 0 340 19510) (A history of the New Zealand offshore station, Radio Hauraki)

Some Useful Addresses

Offshore Echos Magazine PO Box 1514, London W7 2LL
Published five times a year – news and nostalgia about offshore radio worldwide

Radio Review and TV Flashback PO Box 46, Romford, Essex RM7 8AY
Published approximately every six weeks, news and information about radio, (including offshore) as well as radio and TV nostalgia

Radio Caroline 426 Archway Road, Highgate, London N6 4JH
Broadcasting 24 hours a day on Sky and Worldspace

Radio Caroline Sales 148 Grange Road, Ramsgate, Kent CT11 9PR
Memorabilia – pictures, CDs, books, videos, DVDs etc. about offshore radio and Radio Caroline in particular (all profits go towards restoration of the *Ross Revenge*)

Web sites

There are many web sites dealing with offshore radio, these are just a few to get you started. All these sites also contain links to others dealing with individual stations, DJs, general information, memorabilia, news and nostalgia.

Radio Caroline **www.radiocaroline.co.uk** - news and information about Radio Caroline, presenters and programmes, memorabilia and nostalgia.

Radio London **www.radiolondon.co.uk** - nostalgia and news about Big L – and many other stations too.

Pirate Radio Hall of Fame **www.offshoreradio.co.uk** - information about stations, DJs – and much more besides

Pirate Radio Sales **www.pirateradiosales.co.uk** - memorabilia for sale and live internet radio station playing the music of the 60's and 70's

Radio 270 Tribute Pages **www.davesden.fsnet.co.uk/r270-00.htm** a site dedicated to this 60's offshore radio station.

Offshore Echo's Magazine **www.offshoreechos.com** - news about offshore radio and personalities, nostalgia and information, memorabilia for sale.

Index

Aherne, Mike 38
Allan, Tony 80
Allbeury, Ted 33-35, 53, 58, 59, 63, 65- 67, 77
Allen, Don 81, 86, 87
Allen, Mike 37
Allen, Vince (Rusty) 80
Amalgamated Broadcasting Co. 5
Animals, The 13, 31
Archer, Andy 87
Asher, Dave 95
Ashley, Simon 30
Associated Press 28

Batchelors, The 30
Bate, Terry 60, 67, 72, 82
Bates, Roy 36-41, 57-59, 71-74
BBC 1, 2, 4-6, 15, 21, 28, 35, 44, 57, 61, 62, 68-70, 74, 83, 84
BBMS 58, 59, 71
Beatles, The 31
Bevins, Reginald 10, 13-15, 17
Birch, Philip 27, 28, 54, 57, 73, 77, 79
Blackburn, Tony 15, 47, 84
Borkum Riff 7
Brady, Pete 29
Britain Radio 49-53, 57, 61, 63, 65-67, 71
Broadside 68
Brown, Ross 80
Bryan, Paul 69

Calvert, Dorothy 55, 57, 63, 64
Calvert, Reg 22, 24, 25, 36-40, 54-56
Capitol Radio 89
Caroline, MV 10-12, 14, 17-21 30, 42, 77, 81, 83, 84, 86, 87, 90
Caroline Television 90
Carrington, Arthur 10
Cash Casino 60
Cheeta 2 46, 47, 53, 54, 57, 65
Churchill, Sir Winston 31
Chicago, Peter 94
City and County Commercial Radio 42, 64
Clark, Christopher 74
Clark, Petula 31
CNBC 4, 6
Cole, Edward 74
Comet 43-44, 57, 58, 64, 65, 80
Communicator 92-94
Conway, Carl 12
Cornucopia 22, 23

Crawford, Allan 6-9, 11, 17, 20, 42
CRLA 67
Curtis, Jack 66, 70

Daily Sketch 15
Dale, Robbie 79, 81, 88
Dannaher, Tom 66
David 30
Day, Roger 52, 86, 87
DCR 3
Dean, Larry 52
Dee, Simon 11, 12, 14, 15, 19
Denham, Lord 70
Duncan, Ronald 73

Ellambar Investments Ltd 48
EMI 15
Estuary Radio Ltd 34, 58, 59, 63, 74
Evans, Charles 25, 30, 33

Fame, Georgie 9, 12
Fredericia 9, 10
Free Radio Association 67, 68

Galaxy 27-29, 45, 73, 79, 87, 89
Gale, Roger 37, 43
GBLN 4 - 6, 25
GBOK 4 - 6
Goodwin Sands 95, 96
Gordon, Jim 87
Gorst, John 62
Granada TV 16
Greenore 9-11, 19, 87
Griffiths, Eldon 57
Guardian, The 15

Hayes, Mike 79
Hearne, Bill 60
Home Service (BBC) 74

Independent Local Radio (ILR) 92, 93, 95
Isle of Man 11, 21, 22, 42, 59, 73, 77, 78, 81, 86
ITU 14

Jeanine 90
Jeeves, Peter 40
Johnson, Duncan 54
Jones, Tom 31

Kaye, Paul 79
Kemp, Garry 37
Kennedy, John F 7, 10
Kerr, Doug 19, 37
King David 89
KING Radio 33-35, 40
King, Terry 24
KLIF 3, 27, 29, 50
Knock John Fort 36-40, 58, 59, 71

Lady Dixon 4, 6
Laissez Faire 50-52, 61, 65-67, 77
Laser 558 92, 93
Laser Hot Hits 93
Leighton, Jerry 19
Light Programme (BBC) 1, 2, 32, 37, 63, 61, 74, 84
Local Radio Association 62
Lodge, Tom 19, 38, 59
Lucky Star 7, 14
Luvzit, Mick 61
Lye, David 33, 63, 74

McDonald, Roy 82
McLendon, Gordon 27
Magda Maria 6 - 8
Magdelena 91
Maitland, Dennis 54
Major Minor 47, 82, 84
Manx Radio 21, 22, 78
Marine Investment Co 27
Marine Offences Act 71, 74, 77-83, 87, 91
Marine Offences Bill 57, 58, 65, 67-71, 72, 73, 77, 78
Martin, Caroline 95
Mebo II 89
Merit Music Publishing 6
Mi Amigo 8-11, 17, 41, 42, 45-47, 59, 60, 72, 80, 81, 83, 86, 87, 90- 92
Mid Atlantic Films 82
Miller, Noel 48
Moore, Christopher 11, 12
Moreno, Ed 5, 29, 30
Musicians Union 15, 62

National Advertiser 68
News of the World 15, 29
Norderney 90

Oceaan VII 48-50, 77, 79, 80, 87
Offshore I 45, 73
Offshore II 73
Offshore III 73
Olga Patricia 50

O'Rahilly, Ronan 9-13, 20, 28, 38, 41, 46, 47, 59, 60, 67, 71, 77, 82, 85, 87, 88, 90

PAMS 51
Panavess Inc 27
Parrish, Leslie 20
People, The 15
Pepper, Tom 25, 29, 33
Phonographic Performances Ltd 14
Pierson, Don 27
Pier Vick 65, 66
Planet Productions Ltd 9, 41, 42, 48
Progressiva Compania Commercial SA 48
Project Atlanta 6 - 11, 14, 17, 41, 42, 54, 59
Proudfoot, Wilf 47, 48, 57, 77

Queen Magazine 20

Radio 227   67, 73, 77
Radio 242   68, 65
Radio 270   38, 47-50, 57, 68, 70, 71, 73, 77-80, 91
Radio 355   66, 67, 73, 75, 77
Radio 390   34, 35, 40, 50-54, 57-59, 63-67, 73, 74, 77
Radio 558   94
Radio 819   94
Radio Albatros 58
Radio Antwerpen 3
Radio Atlanta 4, 17-24, 27, 38, 54, 82
Radio Atlantis 90,91
Radio Caroline 1, 4, 10-32, 36-43, 45-54, 57-62, 68-72, 77-96
Radio City 25, 27, 30, 36-42, 50, 54-59, 63, 64
Radio Delmare 91
Radio Dolfijn 61, 65, 67
Radio ELB 4
Radio England 49-52, 57, 61, 65, 92
Radio Essex 39-40, 57, 58, 71
Radio Four (BBC) 74
Radio Invicta 25-30, 33, 35, 37
Radio Kent 58
Radio LN 4
Radio London 27-32, 36, 37, 41, 42, 45, 47, 50, 53, 54, 57, 59, 61, 68-77, 79-84, 85, 89, 92
Reuters 28
Radio Luxembourg 1-4, 9, 15, 61
Radio Manchester 54
Radio Mercur 3, 7, 14
Radio Mi Amigo 90, 91
Radio Monique 92-94
Radio News 68
Radio Nord 3, 6- 8, 19, 27

Radio Northsea International (RNI) 89-91
Radio One (BBC) 74, 84, 88, 89, 92
Radio Scotland 38, 43, 44, 47, 57, 58, 61, 64, 65, 70, 71, 73, 80
Radio Scotland and Ireland 64, 65
Radio Seagull 90, 91
Radio Sutch 22-26
Radio Syd 3, 46, 53, 57, 65
Radio Three (BBC) 74
Radio Tower 40
Radio Two (BBC) 74, 84
Radio Veronica 3, 4, 7, 63, 88 - 91
Raven, Mike 33
Rawlinson, Sir Peter 58, 59, 63
Red Sands Fort 25, 29, 30, 33-35, 38, 53, 57-59, 63, 67, 74
Reveille 27, 35
Ross Revenge 92-96
Roughs Tower 38, 71, 72

Sealand 72, 76
Scott, Roger 87
Shaw, Martin 30
Shields, Tommy 43, 64, 80
Shivering Sands Fort 23, 24, 27, 36-38, 41, 54, 55, 64
Short, Edward 56, 62, 69, 70, 73
Short, George 39
Skues, Keith 54
Slaight, Alan 60
Smedley, Major Oliver 40, 41, 54, 55, 59, 63
Smethwick, Jerry 52
Soloman, Philip 47, 77, 81, 82, 87
Sorenson, Lord 70
Spector, Jack 32
Spectrum Radio 95
Spencer, Bob 65
Stevens, Gary 57
Strasbourg Convention 31, 56, 69
Sullivan, Eric 39
Sun, The 28
Sunk Head Fort 38, 40, 83
Sutch 'Screaming Lord' David 22-23, 38
Swanson, Arnold 4, 6
Sydney, Jon 37

Tack, Sylvan 90
Third Programme (BBC) 74
Thompson, John 4, 25, 30, 33
Time and Tide 68
Times, The 15, 83
Titan 86
Tongue Sands Fort 38, 58
Tower Radio/TV 39, 40, 83

Turner, Alan 19
Tynwald 21, 77, 78

UKGM 54
United Press International 28
Utrecht 86

van Dam, Gerard 90
Venturous, HMS 14
Vick, Bill 57
Vision Productions 39, 40
Voice of America 28
Voice of Slough 4, 5, 25

WABC 49
Wadner, Britt 3, 46, 53
Walker, Johnnie 80, 81, 86, 90
Walton Lifesaving Apparatus Co 45
Wedgewood Ben, Anthony 30, 55, 56
Wesley, Mark 80
Wijsmuller Tendering Co. 20, 73, 86, 87, 90
WINS 49
Windsor, Tony 77
Wilson, Harold 80, 81
Wireless Telegraphy Act 58, 64
WMCA 32, 49, 51
Woburn Abbey 15
World Mission Radio 94